HOLIDAY COOKIES & CENTERPIECES

THE
BROWNSTONE
LIBRARY

HOLIDAY COOKIES

Allen D. Bragdon Publishers, Inc.
New York

& CENTERPIECES

Creative Ways with Gingerbread

Project Design and Construction:
Barbara Arneborn —*Formal Tea* (designed by P.S. Krosnick Studio), *Monster's Picnic, Noah's Ark, Circus Train, Children's Village, Traditional Ornaments;* Monica Barnouw and Carolyn Ringland—*Easter's Eggs, Swedish Ornaments;* Dottie Brush—*Three Little Pigs, Thanksgiving, Valentine Box, Traditional Ornaments;* Lia Smirlis Chavey—*Saltbox House* (originally published in *Early American Life*); Jim Fobel—*Spooksticks;* Joanne Hayes—*Games, House of Cats, The Dragon's Mountain* (marionettes and story), *Three Little Red Riding Bears* house (figures designed by Mejo Okon); Karo Corn Syrup—*Country Farm, Victorian Carolers, Grandma's House, Village Church* (originally published in *Early American Life*); Kingsford and Argo's Corn Starch—*Window Trimmings* (designed by P.S. Krosnick Studios); Eileen Negrycz—*Gift-wrapped Goodies, The Witch's Cottage;* Larry Rosenberg—*Haunted House;* Real Estate Pages: "Candy Cathedral" and "Cookie Hall" courtesy of Louis Lichtman; "Bavarian Chalet" courtesy of Peter Brandl; "Washington House" and "Victorian Brick" by Tina Strepko, "Strasburg Inn" and "Pretzel Log Chalet" courtesy of Pennsylvania Gingerbread House Invitational sponsored by Historic Strasburg Inn, Lancaster County, PA.

Photography
All photography by Laszlo Studios, New York, except the following: Ornaments—Bird by Frank Moscati; Chanticleer, Austrian I.H.S., St. Nicholas by Peter Brandl. *Real Estate*—"Candy Cathedral" and "Cookie Hall" by Louis Lichtman; "Bavarian Chalet" by Peter Brandl; all others courtesy of Historic Strasburg Inn, Lancaster County, PA. *Cover*—Photo by Laszlo, reprinted courtesy of *Modern Maturity* magazine and Karo Corn Syrup.

Acknowledgements
The following individuals and other sources contributed recipes: Sybil Claiborne; *Early American Life* magazine December 1983; Argo and Kingsford's Corn Starch; Karo Corn Syrup; Graff, *Pfeffernuss und Mandelkern; Mystic Seaport Cookbook;* The Pomona Grange; Spicer, *From an English Oven;* Aline Steyer
We would like to thank others whose efforts made a difference in the content and production of this book: Nancy Colestock and Frances Carnahan at *Early American Life;* Sherrill McGoldrick and Susan Plump at Best Foods U.S., CPC International; Cathy Farmer at Historic Strasburg Inn; Anthony Y. Wang of Laszlo Studios; Mr. and Mrs. Bosboom of H. Roth and Son; Peter Choy of Bookbuilders, Ltd., Hong Kong; Christine Brandl; Mr. and Mrs. Kenneth Stouffer; Peter von Ziegesar, Chris and Mary Toy.

Staff for this book:
Editor in Chief—Allen D. Bragdon
Senior Editor—Hannah Selby
Associate Editors— Amanda Claiborne, Karen Johnsen
Designer—Mejo Okon
Layout Associate—Michael Eastman
Graphic Production—Conrad Warre
Illustrations—Carol Winter
Historical Introduction—Maureen Graney

Designed, Produced, and Published by
Allen D. Bragdon Publishers, Inc.
153 West 82nd Street
New York, NY 10024

Distributed to the retail book trade by
Kampmann & Company
9 East 40th St., New York 10016
Originally published in hardcover edition
as The Gingerbread Book.

Library of Congress Cataloging in Publication Data
Holiday cookies & centerpieces.
  (The Brownstone library)
  Rev. ed. of: The Gingerbread book. c1984.
  1. Gingerbread. 2. Gingerbread houses.
I. Bragdon, Allen D. II. Gingerbread book.
TX771.H68 1986   745.5   86-23316
ISBN 0-916410-37-4 (pbk.)

Printed in Hong Kong

Contents

Introduction

The best thing about gingerbread, like affection, is the sharing. People create gingerbread houses to make other people smile—even construct them with the help of other people sometimes.

Another gentle fact about gingerbread is that its ingredients and the tools one needs do not cost much. Memorable gingerbread houses are made with patience and imagination, not with expensive equipment. Fortunately, gingerbread construction is not yet one of the popular TV sports. (Those often make the personality of the doer more important than the thing done, or lead people to believe that the gleaming equipment they buy is more important than the quiet time they take to try doing something well. That just is not so.)

Also, there is something historically mysterious about gingerbread—it's like honey that way. Ginger, and cookies flavored with it, have been appearing in accounts of ordinary people's daily lives since the beginning of written history. Decorative shapes seem always to have been part of the picture. Because the commanding flavor of ginger attracts the palate's attention so forcefully, the creator of the cookie can let flavor take care of itself and express a personal touch in the decoration.

A gingerbread house is not just a square cookie with a roof. It is a three-dimensional chuckle of appreciation—a focus for feeling good. Even Hansel and Gretel's witch knew that. In fact,

the dramatic surprise of Hansel and Gretel's predicament is that gingerbread has always been for friends. Nobody wants to make a batch of cookies, shape them, decorate them with frosting, arrange them on a pretty plate, then sit down and eat them all alone. Well, almost nobody.

A warm, thick, steamy-dark cake-pan of gingerbread right out of the oven, cut quickly into cubes, lifted out onto plates, and served up with a fork and a pitcher of lemon sauce, that's what memories are made of—so were those tingle-tongued, snapping-crisp ginger cookies made by your grandmother's sister because she knew you might come to visit—and so was the first gingerbread house you ever saw, lovingly made and put out on the table where you could see it when you walked in the door. Those are things people do because they, privately and personally, want someone to grin. This is so personal a medium, gingerbread, that it is almost a shame to make a book about it.

Still, a memorable party is worth a thousand words, and with luck, there may be some ideas in here you can use to broaden a smile. Like any written-down collection compiled by experts for interested peers, at the very least this book will be a stimulating place to take off from toward a refreshing idea of your own that's going to be worth the doing. We hope your children like the fairy tales.

—Allen Bragdon, Editor

The History of Gingerbread

It has been baked in Europe for centuries. In some places, it was a soft cake, in others, a brittle cookie. It was sometimes light, sometimes dark, sometimes sweet, sometimes spicy, but almost always it was cut into shapes and colorfully decorated, or stamped with a mold and dusted with white sugar to make the impression visible. We have inherited gingerbread from many old times and many old places and its history is filled with traditions we have made our own.

TAKE ME TO THE FAIR

If you lived in London in 1614, your family would have gone to the Bartholomew Fair on August 24th. You might have gone there to buy a winter's worth of cloth, but the children would have tugged you to the puppet show, begged you to let them see Lantern Leatherhead's hobbyhorses and toys, and scampered among the carts and trays of the noisy, wandering costermongers looking for one special peddler. Then they would hear her cry:

Buy any gingerbread!
Gilt Gingerbread!

There she was, Joan Trash, the gingerbread woman! The children would run up to her, peek over the rim of her basket, and their eyes would widen at what they saw: little gilded figures of men, women, animals, saints—especially many of St. Bartholomew, whose feast day the fair celebrated—all in gingerbread! You surely would have bought some of the gingerbread woman's wares. But if you

had been nearby a few moments earlier you would have heard the hobbyhorse seller muttering to anyone within earshot that Joan Trash's gingerbread was made with "stale bread, rotten eggs, musty ginger, and dead honey." If you lived in 1614, you would have known the recipe to be accurate but would have shrugged off the insult.

Country fairs in England were rowdy places where whole towns traded, played, ate, danced, drank, and sang. Roguish merchants made a high art out of shouting colorful insults about each other's wares, trying to call attention to their own. Frequently they ended up in the special pie-powders court—(court of dusty feet—where petty grievances were settled). The shouting matches among the merchants were just a colorful show, certainly nothing that would keep anyone away from the gingerbread basket.

But what about the strange ingredients Lantern Leatherhead described? In reality, he and Joan Trash are just characters in Ben Jonson's play *Bartholomew Fair*, but there is nothing imaginary about the fair or about that recipe.

Of the special cakes prepared for holidays and feasts in England, many were gingerbread. If a fair honored a town's patron saint, that saint's image might have been stamped into the gingerbread you would buy. If the fair was a special market day, the cakes would probably be decorated with an edible icing to look like men, animals, valentine hearts, or flowers. Sometimes the dough was simply cut into round "snaps."

Brown, gingery "fair buttons," for example, were baked for the Easter Pleasure Fair in Norwich and the Easter and pre-Lenten fair in nearby Great Yarmouth. A kind of gingerbread stick that was a little like shortbread was traditional at the Ashbourne Fair in Derbyshire on the first Sunday after August 16th. Gingerbread wafers were eaten with cheese, sweets, and spiced ale at the mid-September Barnstable Fair in Devonshire. Little cones and tubes made out of gingerbread were hawked in the streets of Nottingham during the great "goose fair," when thousands of geese were driven into the town and people came from all over to choose a Christmas goose. And in Yorkshire on Christmas eve, the festive atmosphere in homes spilled out into the streets, and children went from house to house visiting, singing, and begging for pennies and bits of Yule cake, spice cake, or pepper cake.

A PENNYWORTH OF GINGER

Gingerbread in the England of Shakespeare and Ben Jonson was made out of breadcrumbs, honey, and spices. Red and white wine, ale, and brandy were also commonly called for in recipes. A cookbook published in 1615 gives the full details of how "a course Gingerbread" was made in those days:

> Take a quart of honie and set it on the coales and refine it: then take a pennyworth of ginger, as much peper, as much Licoras, and a quarter of a pound of Aniseedes, and a penny worth of Saunders [red sandalwood]: All these must be heaten and seared, and so put up the hony: then put in a quarter of a pint of claret

wine or old Ale: then take three penny Manchets [the best kind of white bread] finely grated and strow it amongst the rest; and stirre it till it come to a stiffe Past, and then make it into Cakes and drie them gently. (Gervase Markham, *The English Hus-wife.*)

Gradually, molasses and flour replaced the honey and breadcrumbs, making a dark, rich gingerbread that became part of the lively street life in English cities. Throughout the eighteenth and nineteenth centuries, the wandering gingerbread vendors called:

> *Hot spice-gingerbread, hot!*
> *hot! all hot!*
> *Come, buy my spice-*
> *gingerbread, smoking hot!*

or

> *Hot spiced gingerbread nuts,*
> *nuts, nuts!*
> *If one'll warm you,*
> *wha-a-a-t'll a pound do!*

At the weekday markets, where working people bought their meals, or the Saturday night markets, where they bought victuals for Sunday dinner, the gingerbread seller was a noisy, irresistible presence. He tempted children with "toy gingerbread" images from street life: the "cock in breeches" with "nether garments" of gold (cock fighting in those days was a popular entertainment); or "king George on Horseback," who had a gilt crown, spurs, sword, and whose horse had a gilded saddle. Animals lent their shapes to gingerbread, too, and sheep and dogs were favorites. The London Johnny Boy, another baked figure, was not made out of gingerbread but of regular bread dough. Nonetheless, he probably inspired our stories about the gingerbread man. His little legs were so springy that he was said to have once sprung out of the oven and escaped. Gingerbread-making was eventually recognized as a profession in itself. In the seventeenth century, gingerbread bakers had the exclusive right to make it, *except* at Christmas and Easter. Their street cries could be heard well into the nineteenth century, but in 1851, the writer Henry Mayhew recorded sadly that "there are only two men in London who make their own gingerbread nuts for sale in the streets."

LEBKUCHEN TO PAIN D'EPICES

If you lived in Nuremberg in 1614, your family would have gone to the *Christkindlmarkt* in December. You would have bought carved Christmas decorations, special sausages, and the famous Nuremberg *Lebkuchen*, which you probably would have thought was the best in the world. And even if you had never had gingerbread anywhere else, you just might have been right. For years, bakers in Nuremberg had access to a selection of ingredients few European cities could rival. Sugar in medieval Europe was rare and expensive. But in Nuremberg, honey flowed in abundance because groups of beekeepers had settled in the woods surrounding the city and brought their honey into town to sell in the markets. Spices were usually hard to get (pepper and ginger were the only spices that regularly appeared in English household spice records in the thirteenth century, for example) but Nuremberg was a junction of trade routes from Hungary in the east and Venice and the Mediterranean in the south. All kinds of spices were commonplace there. Nuremberg merchants, in fact, were so well known for their spices that they had the nickname "pepper sacks." From early on, Nuremberg's *Lebkuchen* packed into one recipe all the variety of flavorings available to its bakers—cardamom, cloves, cinnamon, white pepper, anise, and ginger.

Nuremberg was such a powerful trading center that it attracted and motivated a class of master craftspeople who wanted to be where they could get raw materials in exchange for their finished products. There were tinfounders, diecutters, sculptors, painters, woodcutters, goldsmiths. The bakers too took pride in their craft. *Lebkuchen* bakers, who elaborately decorated their cakes with whole cloves and colorful icing, saw themselves as artisans. Maybe wood engravers inspired them to carve forms for pressing patterns into their gingerbread; maybe the goldsmiths provided them with gold dust for their edible golden paints. Did you know that the first printed cookbook was produced there in 1485, and it contained recipes for golden cookie paint, for food coloring of many hues, and it talked about *Lebkuchen*.

Gingerbread and *Pfeffernüsse*, literally, pepper nuts, were produced a little differently in each town and by each family. To some, almonds and candied citrus peel were as standard as the ginger. Sometimes the recipes did not even include ginger; then, pepper or anise gave the cakes their flavor. But among German-speaking people, as well as in France, *Lebkuchen*, *Pfeffernüsse*, and *pain d'épices* have always been essentially honey cakes. The German word *Lebkuchen* came from the Latin *libum*, the name of a special pancake that was spread with honey and offered to the Roman gods (much the way our word "libation" came from a Latin word meaning to make a liquid offering). The French *pain d'épices* means, literally, bread of spices.

The traditions in France were closer to the German than the English ones, with noteworthy recipes for *pain d'épices* coming from Dijon, Reims, and Paris. In 1571, French bakers of *pain*

d'épices even won the right to their own guild, or professional organization, separate from the other pastry cooks and bakers.

GINGER AS MEDICINE

Gingerbread has always been a delicacy, not quite in a category with everyday breads and pastries or even other holiday cakes. Its almost magical appeal has probably been passed on since the Europeans' first experiences with the spice when, in the Middle Ages, it was used medicinally. In the thirteenth century, apothecaries kept supplies of it. As a hot and dry substance, it could counteract an imbalance among the four humors that, in medieval medicine, were supposed to control a person's health and temperament. Later, it was believed to relieve respiratory difficulties, strengthen weak stomachs, and expel plague, and was combined in electuaries (confections) with honey. It was also used as a food preservative—to "resist Putrefaction," according to a 1725 English translation of the Frenchman Pierre Pomet's *Compleat History of Druggs*. In fact, gingerbread did not spoil as quickly as other baked goods, which, in the days before refrigeration, was certainly somewhat magical. Gingerbread went to battle with many an army and sailed with many a ship.

ENTER THE GINGERBREAD HOUSE

During the nineteenth century, gingerbread was both modernized and romanticized. When the Grimm brothers collected volumes of German fairy tales, they found one about Hansel and Gretel, two children who, abandoned in the woods by destitute parents, discovered a house made of bread, cake, and candies. By the end of the century, the composer Englebert Humperdink wrote an opera about the boy and the girl and the gingerbread house.

Meanwhile, people in the Victorian age in England and America, and the parallel Biedermeier era, began to turn away from the colorful, bustling street-life that had been such an important part of daily life during the medieval and Elizabethan periods. As people turned to the private havens of their own homes, gingerbread came off the street into the kitchen. Perhaps at the same time people were inspired by the romantic Hansel and Gretel opera story to bake square cookies and construct houses decorated with candies like those the lost children plucked from the roof and windows of the witch's cottage.

ANIMAL COOKIES

Factories were the reality of late nineteenth-century Europe, and the production of gingerbread became an industry. But some romanticism remained: when books were published in Germany and France evaluating baking machinery, they did not neglect gingerbread history. One shows intricate molds for fancy single cookies. Another shows a cutter that was like a watermelon-sized rolling pin and pressed relief ducks, lambs, roosters, flowers, houses, castles, horses, lords, and ladies into square cookies—albeit hundreds at a time. Smaller rolling cutters of a similar design are still made.

England had been exporting animal-shaped cookies to America since the mid 1800s, by which time Americans had developed an appetite for fancy baked goods. We don't know whether the animals were ginger-spiced, but by the 1870s, animals were being baked in New York and eventually became the famous American animal crackers in the bright circus boxes.

AMERICAN TASTE

By the nineteenth century, America had been baking gingerbread for decades. Although instructions for gingerbread in Martha Washington's recipe book were very close to the breadcrumb recipe of 1615, the first cookbook printed in the new nation called for molasses and flour, which were the ingredients then used in England. That book, written by Amelia Simmons in 1796, instructs the reader to shape the dough "to your fancy." American cookbooks tended to encourage the baker's creativity more than the English cookbooks of the time, which usually just recommended cutting rolled dough with the rim of a glass. *The New England Cookery Book* of 1808 notes that dough can be stamped or cut out, and *The Virginia Housewife* says "plebian Gingerbread" should be cut into shapes.

Thus began a flexible, creative gingerbread tradition. American recipes usually called for fewer spices than their European counterparts, but often made use of ingredients that were only available regionally. Maple syrup gingerbreads were made in New England, and in the South, sorghum molasses was used. Waves of new immigrants added their own recipes to the American repertoire, and in 1898, *The Golden Age Cookbook* listed recipes for eleven spice cakes, among them *Lebküchen* made with honey, orange peel, and rum; a ginger layer cake using "porto Rico" molasses; gingerbread made with sour cream; and a spiced honey cake from Norway. All gingerbread makers recall the whole joyful, colorful history of gingerbread both in what they make and how they make it.

So now, you live in the 1980s and you can flavor, shape, and decorate your gingerbread as you like it.

An I had but one penny in the world, thou should'st have it to buy ginger-bread."
—William Shakespeare
Love's Labours Lost

CELEBRATIONS

CONTENTS

Easter's Eggs

The exquisitely-decorated, miniature hollow eggs created by the master jeweler to the Russian court, Peter Carl Fabergé, inspired the 8-inch gingerbread replica on this page. Overleaf is a traditional Ukrainian "pysanka" with its interlocking geometric design, typical of the mountain regions of the Ukraine. The floral motif for the hollow egg opposite reflects the renewing freshness of the Easter season.

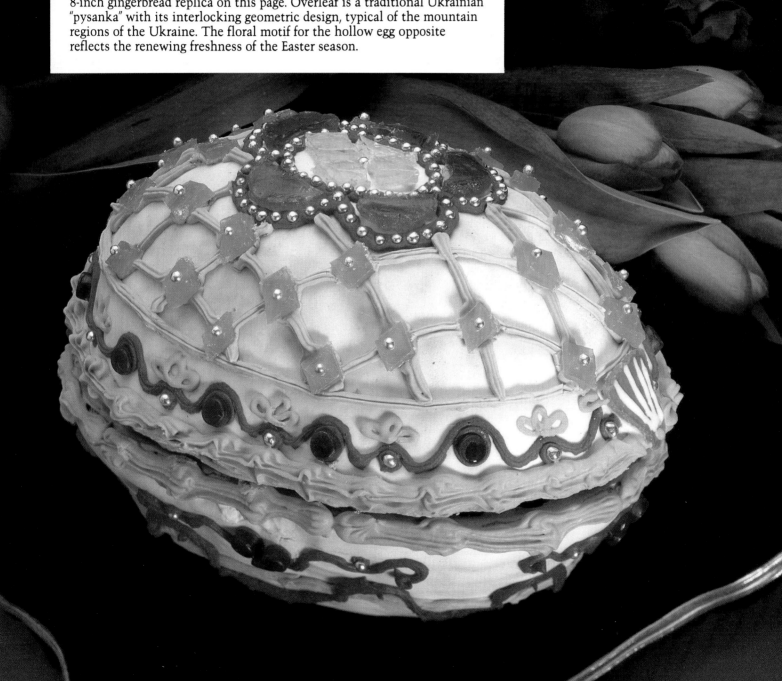

This project consists of three hollow eggs made from six halves baked on molds, each measuring approximately 5 x 8 inches. They will be decorated in the styles of Fabergé, bejeweled and glazed with an assortment of candies; Ukrainian, frosted in one of the geometric designs typical of this region; and Floral, decorated in spring-like Easter colors. Two Easter bunny shapes are decorated in 20 different patterns and colors. A string of "gingerbeads" is threaded as soon as they are cool enough to touch, then glazed when hardened.

Grouped together in a straw basket, or displayed individually, these unusual eggs lend themselves to a variety of display ideas—brighten an entrance hall table or fireplace mantel, for example. The Fabergé egg, opened to display a string of glazed gingerbread beads, makes a spectacular centerpiece for a sideboard or dining table. For a special Easter treat for six people, nestle each open egg-half in yellow paper "grass" on a doily-covered plate and fill it with an Easter gift of cookies, chocolates, or fresh flowers. For an Easter morning that a young child won't soon forget, fill the Ukrainian or Floral egg with a collection of small decorated gingerbread bunnies and leave it next to the bed as a special, special gift from the Easter Bunny.

This project is rewarding, but challenging. It will go much more quickly, and be more fun, with two pairs of hands. The baking, assembling, and decorating of the eggs (the dough should be mixed the night before the rolling and baking day) *can* be accomplished by two people in two weekends, but three weekends would be more comfortable.

A SHORT HISTORY OF FABERGÉ

One of the most famous jewelers of all time, Peter Carl Fabergé is probably best known for his fanciful and ingenious Imperial Easter Eggs, commissioned by Czar Alexander III for his ailing wife. The son of a jeweler, Fabergé was born in 1846 in St. Petersburg (now Leningrad). He was popular with royal families throughout Europe and the Far East, and was particularly noted for his enamel work and unprecedented combinations of materials: metals, precious jewels, and stones. He delighted in the unexpected, often including a mechanical device or some ingenious surprise element in his designs.

The Russian Revolution brought confusion and upheaval and Fabergé's shop was taken over to manufacture war arms. He continued making his eggs and other creations, however, until he was forced to flee the country. He died in 1920 in Lausanne and with him his great firm, the House of Fabergé, came to an end.

UKRAINIAN EASTER EGGS ("PYSANKA")

This unique method of egg coloring developed in the Slavic countries where decorating eggs has long been a popular tradition, especially at Easter time. Using a wax-resist technique similar to batik fabric dyeing, the Easter Eggs are decorated with various designs, ranging from geometric to floral, depending on the region of the country. Each village also produces its own designs, such as fir trees, priests' robes, bell towers, horses, and flowers. The eggs are generally given away as gifts—from families to their priests, or young women to their beaus—and are saved and treasured as heirlooms.

YOU WILL NEED:

See Basic Skills chapter for general equipment and materials.

Oval-shaped metal mold (or any oven-proof mold or bowl) that closely resembles half of an egg in shape. Dimensions should be about 4 x 6 inches (the finished egg half will be approximately 5 x 8 inches). If you want to bake 2 halves at the same time, have on hand 2 molds or bowls. Stands for eggs, if to be displayed separately, should be circular and about 1-inch wide and 3 inches in diameter. You can use small, simple children's bracelets. Or, cut sections off a wide cardboard tube, then glaze with Flow Frosting and decorate to suit your taste.

Heavy-duty foil, vegetable cooking spray (optional), pastry brush, buttonhole twist thread, 2 (or more) small bunny cookie cutters, pastry bags (as many as needed for different icing colors), cake decorator tips #'s 2, 3, 14, 30, 47.

Assorted candies:
1 dozen jelly candies in jewel tone colors
1 jar silver and/or gold decors (small balls)
¼ pound small French mints in different pastel colors
Any other small gem-like candies which are suitable for decorating and produce a jeweled look

1 batch Royal Icing (make more as needed); Flow Frosting

MIXING THE DOUGH
8 ounces margarine or butter
3 cups sugar
1 cup molasses
3 tablespoons ginger
1 tablespoon cloves
1 egg
2 tablespoons baking soda
1 cup heavy cream
9 cups flour

1. Melt margarine in a large stainless steel saucepan, then add sugar, molasses, and spices and stir over low heat until well blended.
2. Stir in egg and baking soda (mixture will froth slightly).
3. Add heavy cream and stir until well blended.
4. Remove from heat and stir in flour. You may find it easier to work the last cup of flour into the mixture with your hands.
5. Cover dough and refrigerate several hours or overnight.

Yield: this recipe makes enough dough for 10 egg halves, 90 to 100 beads, and 4 dozen small bunny cookies.

CUTTING AND BAKING THE EGGS
1. On floured work surface, roll out a

handful of dough to ⅛-inch thickness. You will use about ¾ of the dough for 6 egg halves.

2. Cover mold with heavy-duty aluminum foil, then spray it with vegetable cooking spray or grease it and dust lightly with flour.

3. Place mold on a plate or tray, then drape rolled-out dough on mold, allowing dough to extend about ½-inch beyond bottom edge of mold. This will make it easier to trim edge of egg after baking.

4. Place mold in freezer for about 10 minutes before baking.

5. Line cookie sheet with aluminum foil and spray it with vegetable cooking spray or grease it, then place mold on foil.

6. Bake at 350°F for 10 to 12 minutes or until a golden brown. Remove from oven.

7. While still warm, carefully remove excess dough from bottom edge of mold with a sharp knife. Do not tear baked dough.

8. Before completely cooled, carefully separate mold from baked egg half, then gently form the ends to resemble an egg shape.

9. Cool for at least 24 hours before decorating.

GLAZING THE EGGS

1. When baked egg halves are completely cooled and hardened, and before you decorate the outside, glaze insides with 2 coats of Flow Frosting, applied with a paint brush. Color frosting to your taste and thin it slightly before applying. Allow at least 4 hours between first and second coats.

2. If you wish, decorate insides of eggs in a motif complementary to the outside decoration.

DECORATING THE EGGS

1. Before decorating outsides of egg halves, glaze with Flow Frosting in your choice of tint and allow to dry completely (at least 4 hours). Of course you can apply decorations directly to the gingerbread without glazing first, if you wish.

2. Draw designs on eggs in pencil before beginning to decorate them, following patterns in book.

Decorate the egg halves using the color photographs and patterns as guides, but exercise your own imagination as well.

Hint: work on only 1 egg half at a time.

3. Put Royal Icing into small bowls and tint in colors you desire.

4. Glue candies to eggs and pipe on various designs using Royal Icing applied in pastry bags fitted with decorator's tips. See Basic Skills chapter for instructions on using pastry bags and selecting proper sized tips.

Hint: to attach the candy, pipe an "X" with a #3 tip to mark the spot, then press candy on egg.

Hint: work on one area of egg half at a time, adding decoration then allowing icing to set about 5 minutes before continuing.

5. Prepare stands for eggs if needed. Note: if using real flowers in Floral Egg, make sure stems are not wet, or line inside of egg with plastic wrap.

MAKING THE GINGER-BEAD NECKLACE

1. Roll small bits of dough between the palms of the hand into balls ³⁄₁₆-inch in diameter (the finished beads will be about ½-inch in diameter). You will use approximately 1 cup of dough for beads.

2. Arrange about 12 beads at a time on a greased cookie sheet and bake at 350°F for 5 minutes.

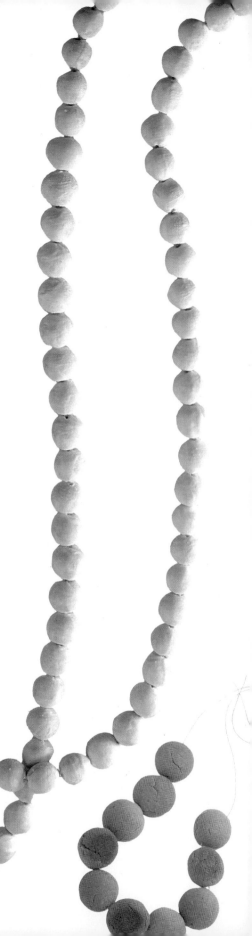

Hint: bake the beads in a toaster oven with a glass door—you can see when they are ready to come out and your oven is left free for other uses.

3. Remove beads from oven and immediately string onto buttonhole twist thread. The needle will go through easily when beads are still warm and have not yet hardened.

4. Allow beads to cool thoroughly before glazing.

5. Make Royal Icing and mix Flow Frosting following recipe in Basic Skills chapter.

6. For glaze, tint Flow Frosting to desired color.

Hint: if you want a necklace with a pearl look, then tint to an off-white—1 or 2 drops of yellow coloring gives this shade. The necklace can also be left "natural" (gingerbread color) if you wish.

7. With soft paint brush, glaze beads on 1 side.

Hint: it's easier if you space beads a bit apart along thread. Allow to dry (about 4 hours), then turn beads over and glaze other half. Dry completely.

8. Glaze each side once more, following step 7, to get a really rich jewel look.

MAKING THE BUNNY COOKIES

1. On floured work surface, roll out a handful of dough to ⅛-inch thickness. You will need about 2 cups of dough for the cookies.

2. Using small bunny cookie cutters, cut out desired number of cookies.

3. Place on greased cookie sheet and bake at 350°F for 5 minutes.

4. Allow cookies to cool, then decorate with Royal Icing, Flow Frosting, and/or candies. Copy the decorative patterns in the color photograph, if you wish.

This is a full-sized pattern for one side of the top half of the Fabergé Easter egg. Since both sides are identical, trace this pattern; transfer it, with carbon paper, to one side of the baked egg half; reverse it to trace the other side.

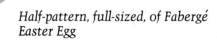

Half-pattern, full-sized, of Fabergé Easter Egg

These are full-sized patterns for one side of the top halves of the Flower Easter egg (blue) and Ukranian Easter egg (yellow). Both sides of each egg are identical.

the
HAUNTED
HOUSE!

Whoooo dares come close enough to peek through the broken panes in the stained glass window? Look out! A licorice tile slipped off the roof (or was it thrown) from the teetering turret? A crystalized ginger stone from the chimney is loose and could crash down any second if you sneak by to look in through the leaded window made of edible gelatin. What, you see a skeleton in the chimney? I don't. But there are blue lights flickering inside and...*I just heard a scream!*

The designer of this Halloween centerpiece has turned the cheerful, chuckly, gingerbread medium into a tower of terror. The house slants, the shutters are broken, the slabs of dough are thick, and the frosting sags in sinister gobs.

The dough recipe, baking instructions, and decorating technique are in the Middle-European tradition—spicy, rolled out thick, and decorated with chunky clumps of icing—the perfect style for a Halloween horror-piece. The back has been left open so you can string tiny blue Christmas tree lights inside with an on-off-on flasher so they will flicker through the windows. Record a terror-tape, or buy one with screams, creaking doors, rattling chains, and owl's who-whoooos on it, and tuck a tiny tape player inside. Just before your guests enter the room, turn on the blue lights, start the tape player, and flick off the light in the room. (If that doesn't get 'em, the Bat Cookies will!)

YOU WILL NEED:
See Basic Skill chapter for general equipment and materials.

In addition, have on hand full food cans, cardboard tubes from paper towels, and thick (sandwich) toothpicks.

3 batches gingerbread dough
1 batch icing
A 12 x 18-inch base of ½-inch plywood
Paste food coloring: black, egg yellow, and brown
Orange liquid food coloring
2 packages sheet gelatin (2 sheets)

Edibles: Salmiak (Dutch licorice), Black peppercorns, Australian crystalized ginger (very soft), Black licorice whips, Black licorice laces, Black licorice chips, Crumbled, dark bittersweet chocolate or ground coffee, Florist's wire, White chocolate, Red nonpareils

MAKING THE PATTERNS
The patterns for The Haunted House are given in reduced dimensions. To make full-sized patterns, use the dimensions indicated.

1. With ruler, T-square, and triangle, make full-sized tracing paper patterns following instructions in Basic Skills chapter.
2. Make and cut out cardboard patterns following instructions in Basic Skills chapter. Be sure to draw door and window openings on pattern pieces and cut them out. Note that H and I are the same width, but I is 2¼ inches longer than H.

MIXING THE DOUGH
Make 3 separate batches. Do not triple.

12 cups unsifted flour
12 tablespoons baking powder
2 tablespoons ground cinnamon
2 teaspoons ground cloves
2 teaspoons ground ginger
½ teaspoon ground cardamom
¼ teaspoon salt
1½ cups honey
3½ cups sugar
½ cup butter
　Juice and grated peel of 1 lemon
2 eggs, extra-large
2 egg yolks, extra-large

1. In large bowl, combine flour, baking powder, cinnamon, cloves, ginger, cardamom, and salt.
2. In a 4- or 5-quart saucepan, bring honey, sugar, and butter to a boil over high heat, stirring with large wooden spoon until sugar is dissolved and butter is melted. Remove from heat and stir in lemon juice and peel. Cool to room temperature.
3. When cool, beat in 6 cups of flour mixture until well blended. Beat in eggs and egg yolks, and then beat in remaining flour mixture.

4. Flour hands and knead dough until it is smooth and pliable but still slightly sticky. If too moist to handle, beat in more flour one tablespoon at a time.

BAKING AND CUTTING
One batch of dough will fill two 12 x 18 x ½-inch jelly roll or strudel pans. You will need to bake 6 pans of dough, so you can prepare and bake 2 at a time. The gingerbread becomes firmer and easier to handle as it ages. Therefore, you can do the baking over a period of several days as long as you cut out the pieces 5 minutes after the dough is baked.

Note: this gingerbread is unusual because it is ½-inch thick. This makes it stronger, especially after the house has dried thoroughly for at least a week.

1. Grease two 12 x 18 x ½-inch pans and line with parchment or waxed paper. Grease and flour paper.
2. Place half the dough in each pan.
3. With a lightly floured rolling pin, press and roll out dough to an even ½-inch thickness, forcing it into corners with your fingers.
4. To make rough-looking walls, push your fist into the dough. The impressions will remain after baking.
5. Bake in preheated oven at 325°F for 40 minutes or until gingerbread is firm and top is brown. Cool in pan 5 minutes.
6. Cut out cookie shapes following instructions in Basic Skills chapter.

Note: unlike other projects in this book, the dough is baked and cooled just 5 minutes, then the shapes are cut out. The basic instructions for cutting out pieces apply, but be very careful when positioning patterns and cutting because the freshly-baked dough is fragile.

Cut 1 piece A with 4 windows and door (for the front) and 1 with a big square hole large enough to pass a small tape recorder through (for the back). Cut 1 piece B with all 4 windows (left side) and the other with only the 2 right-hand windows (right side). Likewise, cut 1 piece D with round window (front) and the other without (back). Be sure to reserve door and window pieces because they will be used to make door and shutters.

7. Very carefully set pieces on waxed paper until they cool completely. The sides are especially fragile due to the cutouts.

8. To make house slant, cut ¼ inch off bottom edge of right house side B and slightly shave right corners of house front and back A.

MAKING THE ICING
    4 egg whites, extra-large
    5 cups confectioners sugar
    2 teaspoons cream of tartar

1. In large bowl (a copper bowl will produce the greatest volume), beat egg whites with whisk or electric mixer at medium speed until they are frothy and slightly thickened.

2. Add confectioners sugar to whites ½ cup at a time, beating thoroughly after each addition. After all sugar is added, beat for 5 minutes until a stiff icing is formed.

3. Divide icing into 2 bowls. Color 1 with black food paste and the other with egg yellow and brown food paste (creating an ochre color), following instructions in Basic Skills chapter.

Note: The Haunted House is decorated as it is assembled.

ASSEMBLING AND DECORATING THE HOUSE
As you assemble the parts of the house, hold pieces in place until set (about 5 minutes) before proceeding to the next step. Remember "allow to dry completely" means you must let iced parts dry at least 4 hours before continuing assembly.

1. With #10 or #12 decorator's tip, pipe icing along bottom and right back edge of house front A; then position on base. Follow instructions in Basic Skills chapter for applying icing with pastry bag or parchment cone and decorator's tip.

2. Pipe icing along bottom and left edge of right house side B and position on base along back edge of A.

3. Pipe icing along bottom and left

edge of house back A and position on base and along back edge of right house side B.

4. Pipe icing along bottom and right edge of left house side B and position on base and along back edges of house back and front A.

5. Ice and position supports C in 3 inside corners of house (all except front right).

6. Prop house in position using full food cans, following instructions in Basic Skills chapter, then allow to dry completely.

MAKING THE STAINED GLASS WINDOWS
1. With scissors, cut out of sheet gelatin 4 x 3-inch rectangles for the house windows, and a 2½ x 3-inch rectangle for the tower window.

2. Using a small paintbrush, paint one side of gelatin with orange liquid food coloring.

3. On other side, pipe leading with black icing and #2 or #3 decorator's tip. Follow pattern in gelatin for house windows. Use the color photograph as your guide for decorating oval tower window.

4. Pipe ochre icing on house windows and position them. Then pipe ochre icing on tower window and position it in tower front F.

5. For broken window effect, tear holes in gelatin.

DECORATING AND ATTACHING THE SHUTTERS AND DOOR
1. Spread ochre icing on walls of house and tower. See Basic Skills chapter for applying icing with a paintbrush or kitchen knife or spatula.

2. Spread black icing on roofs of house and tower.

3. With sharp knife, cut reserved window pieces in half to make shutters, using extra shutter pieces if necessary.

4. Spread black icing on shutters, then ice in place.

Note: shutters must be iced closed on left bottom front window to conceal internal support.

5. Spread black icing on door and decorate with salmiak and peppercorns, using the illustration as a guide. Then ice in place.

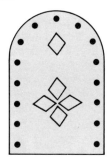

ASSEMBLING THE TOWER AND ROOF
1. Using ochre icing, join tower front and back D and sides E following instructions for assembling the walls of a gingerbread house in Basic Skills chapter.

Note: to strengthen tower, cut remaining support C in half lengthwise. Ice pieces together in an X-shape; then ice to inside of tower.

2. Pipe icing along all edges of tower roofs F and join to top edges of tower front, sides, and back. Don't worry if they don't meet exactly. This will be covered by licorice ridgepole later.

Note: if house roof G has not dried rockhard, you might want to reinforce it before proceeding. Cut a roof piece out of cardboard, spread icing on it, and attach to underside of gingerbread roof.

3. Pipe icing along bottom edges of tower and join to wider part of roof G.

4. Pipe icing along top edges of house and join roof to house. Roof and tower should extend somewhat beyond left side of house. Allow to dry completely.

ASSEMBLING OVERHANGS
To prop overhangs until they dry completely, press thick toothpicks into roof and back of overhangs; then prop bottom of overhangs with cardboard tubes from paper towel rolls.

1. Pipe icing along top edges of front overhang H and side overhang I and join to house roof G. Allow to dry completely.

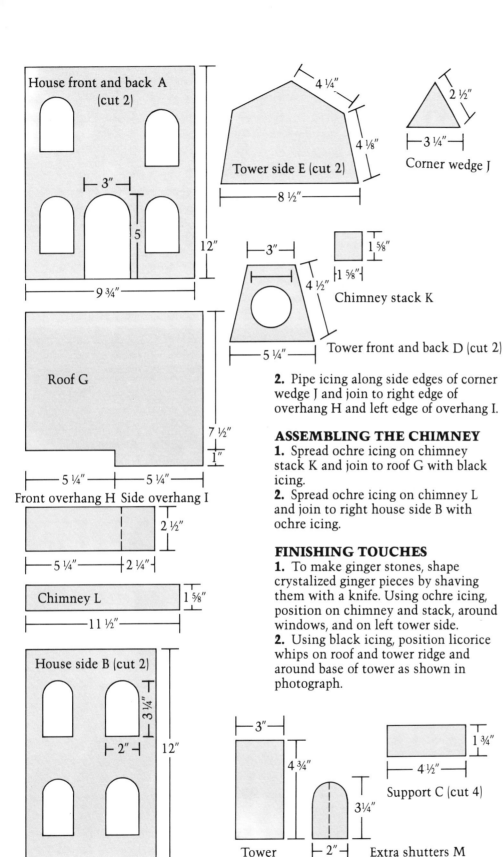

House front and back A (cut 2)

3″

5

12″

9 ¾″

Tower side E (cut 2)

4 ¼″

4 ⅛″

8 ½″

Corner wedge J

2 ½″

3 ¼″

Roof G

7 ½″

1″

5 ¼″   5 ¼″

Front overhang H   Side overhang I

2 ½″

5 ¼″   2 ¼″

Chimney L

1 ⅝″

11 ½″

3″

4 ½″

Chimney stack K

1 ⅝″

1 ⅝″

Tower front and back D (cut 2)

5 ¼″

House side B (cut 2)

3 ¼″

2″

12″

7 ½″

Tower roof F (cut 2)

3″

4 ¾″

Extra shutters M (cut 2)

3 ¼″

2″

Support C (cut 4)

1 ¾″

4 ½″

3. Using black icing, position licorice laces around tower window.
4. Using black icing, position licorice chips on overhangs and roof.
5. For that really "haunted look," make sure that doors and shutters lean crookedly, and that a few roof tiles and stones are loose.
6. Ice a toothpick in black and stick in tower roof.
7. Pipe on cobwebs with black icing and #1 decorator's tip.
8. Spread black icing on base; then, before it dries, sprinkle with crumbled chocolate or ground coffee.
9. Shape tree using licorice whips stiffened with black icing or florist's wire glazed with black icing.
10. Carve a 3 x 1 x ½-inch tombstone of white chocolate and ice it to base. Make a grave mound by heaping crumbled chocolate or ground coffee around tombstone.

2. Pipe icing along side edges of corner wedge J and join to right edge of overhang H and left edge of overhang I.

ASSEMBLING THE CHIMNEY
1. Spread ochre icing on chimney stack K and join to roof G with black icing.
2. Spread ochre icing on chimney L and join to right house side B with ochre icing.

FINISHING TOUCHES
1. To make ginger stones, shape crystalized ginger pieces by shaving them with a knife. Using ochre icing, position on chimney and stack, around windows, and on left tower side.
2. Using black icing, position licorice whips on roof and tower ridge and around base of tower as shown in photograph.

MAKING BAT COOKIES
You should be able to make at least 1½ dozen bat cookies with the extra dough. Use a purchased bat-cookie cutter, or design your own. Leave plain, or ice black with red nonpareils for eyes.

Boo!

YOU WILL NEED:

See Basic Skills chapter for general equipment and materials.

1 pound white chocolate
1 bar milk chocolate

Six 6-inch lengths of ³/₁₆-inch wooden dowel or ice cream sticks

In addition, have on hand: double boiler or saucepans that fit one on top of the other, soup spoon, butter knife.

MAKING THE PATTERNS

1. Make tracing paper patterns following instructions in Basic Skills chapter. You do not make cardboard patterns for this project.

2. Cut a piece of aluminum foil into 6 rectangles slightly larger than the patterns.
3. Place tracing paper patterns over pieces of foil and draw pattern outlines on foil with a pencil. The pressure of the pencil tip will impress the outlines into the foil. Do not cut out foil patterns.

MAKING THE SPOOK STICKS

1. Break white chocolate into 1-inch pieces and place inside top portion of double boiler over hot water.
2. Bring water to simmer over medium heat, then reduce heat to medium low. Cook, stirring occasionally, until chocolate is completely melted.

Note: before proceeding, make sure you have room in either your refrigerator or freezer to hold a cookie sheet.

3. Place foil rectangles on large cookie sheet.
4. Dip wooden sticks into melted chocolate until 2 to 3 inches of them are coated. Vigorously stir melted chocolate each time you use it.
5. Place sticks on foil patterns so chocolate-covered portion is centered within pattern outline.
6. Using a soup spoon, pour melted white chocolate within spook shape.

Hint: for best results, first pour entire outline of shape, then fill in with

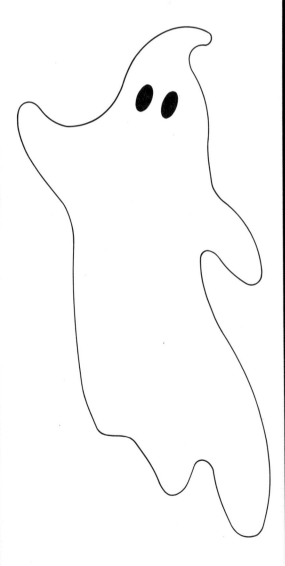

additional melted chocolate.

Note: the white chocolate must remain over hot water the entire time you are working. If chocolate begins to thicken, turn heat up to medium and stir vigorously.

7. Refrigerate or freeze each spook stick on its foil pattern as soon as you finish it. Make all 6 sticks before adding eyes.

MAKING THE EYES

1. Fill the bottom of a double boiler with a small amount of hot water.
2. Break milk chocolate bar into small pieces and place in top of double boiler.
3. Bring water to simmer over medium heat, then reduce heat to medium low.

Cook milk chocolate, stirring occasionally, until completely melted.
4. One at a time, remove chilled spook sticks from refrigerator or freezer.
5. Dip the tip of a butter knife into the milk chocolate and make 2 oval eyes (refer to patterns for placement and size). Return to refrigerator or freezer until ready to serve.
6. Peel off aluminum foil just before serving spook sticks.

SPOOK STICKS

25

The First Thanksgiving

"The Pilgrims, being artisans and farmers, put their first spring and summer to good use. Unlike the indolent gentry at Jamestown, they planted crops, fished, hunted, traded for furs, and improved their housing. When autumn came, they were prepared for their second winter with a comfortable store of supplies. Grateful for a good season, they declared a three-day period of thanksgiving. Massasoit came with ninety of his braves to take part in the festivities. As his contribution he brought game, including five deer, freshly killed. Bradford sent out four men to hunt enough turkeys, duck, and geese to last a week. With feasting, target shooting, and other sports and pastimes, the settlers passed this thanksgiving period right merrily."

The American Heritage History of the Thirteen Colonies.

YOU WILL NEED:

See Basic Skills chapter for general equipment and materials.

1 batch Basic Molasses Gingerbread Dough
1 batch Royal Icing; Flow Frosting

Candy for decorating: candy corn, cinnamon hots, silver dragees, small gumdrops, green jelly beans, nonpareils.

In addition, have on hand metal spatula, pastry bag with #4 metal tip.

Make patterns, mix and roll out dough, cut out cookie pieces and mark design details, and bake the pieces following instructions in Basic Skills chapter. In order to make a flat gingerbread base on which to attach the turkey and pumpkins, also measure and cut a 6 x 7-inch rectangle.

DECORATING

1. Make 1 batch Royal Icing and mix Flow Frosting, following recipes in Basic Skills chapter.
2. Following chart and color photograph, decorate pieces with frosting and candies before assembling.

ASSEMBLING THE TURKEY

1. Using a #4 metal tip on a pastry bag, pipe a small amount of Royal Icing along side edge of body top A, and along top edge of body side B. Place pieces together to form an angle the same as the upper angle of body front C. Hold in place about 5 minutes or until set. Repeat for opposite side of body.
2. Pipe small amount of icing along front edge of body top A and both front edges of body sides B. Position body

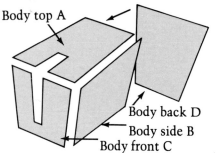

front C against A and B so that slits of A and C line up and side edges of C meet front edges of B. Hold in place until set.
3. Pipe small amount of icing along back edge of A and both backs of B. Position body back D, matching top to back of A and sides to backs of body sides B. Hold in place until set. You now have a 5-sided, somewhat angled box.
4. Pipe small amount of icing along all 4 edges of body bottom E. Position assembled body on top of E. Hold in place about 5 minutes or until set. You now have a 6-sided, somewhat angled box.
5. With metal spatula, spread small amount of icing on surface of body bottom E and properly position on base. Allow to set.
6. With metal spatula, spread back side of inner tail F with icing. Properly position on front of outer tail G, centering and lining up bottoms. Allow to set.

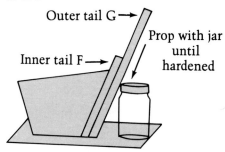

7. With metal spatula, spread small amount of icing on surface of body back D and join assembled tail to body back D, matching up bottom edges. Hold in place until set. Prop with jar until completely dry.

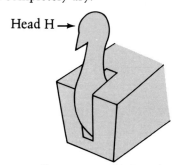

8. Pipe small amounts of icing along

edges of slits in body front and top. Carefully position head H by sliding head H bottom into slit. Hold in upright position until set.
9. To position wings, pipe a small amount of icing in middle of undecorated side of one wing. Carefully position wing along body side B. Back of wing should angle out slightly. Hold in place until set. Repeat for other wing.

ASSEMBLING THE CENTERPIECE

1. Spread Flow Frosting on base. Before frosting dries, sprinkle with crumbled shredded wheat.
2. Pipe small amount of icing on bottom edge of decorated pumpkins. Place pumpkins in proper positions. Hold in place until set.
3. To make figures stand upright, pipe small amount of icing along longest edge of support J and fix at right angle to undecorated side of figure. Hold in place until set.
4. You can make a permanent, unbreakable base for the turkey and other elements of the centerpiece (a good idea if you plan to move it around very much). After you have attached the turkey and pumpkins to the 6 x 7-inch gingerbread base, arrange everything the way you want it, then cut a piece of ¼-inch plywood or other stiff material large enough to hold the entire scene. Conceal the edges with icing, fall foliage, or other decoration.

GINGER APPLE PIE

1 batch of your favorite double crust pastry dough
¾ cup sugar
1 tablespoon cornstarch
½ teaspoon ground ginger
2 pounds apples, peeled, cored, sliced (about 6 cups)
1 tablespoon lemon juice
1 tablespoon butter or margarine

1. Preheat oven to 425°F.
2. Line 9-inch pie plate with half the dough rolled to a circle about 11 inches in diameter and ⅛-inch thick.
3. In large bowl, combine sugar,

cornstarch, and ginger. Add apple slices and lemon juice and toss mixture until apples are well coated.

4. Turn mixture into pie plate and dot top with butter or margarine.

5. Roll out remaining dough to a 12-inch circle ⅛-inch thick, then carefully lay over apple mixture. Seal and flute edges all around.

6. Make several slits in top to permit steam to escape.

7. Bake in 425°F oven 50 minutes or until crust is golden.

MARMALADE APPLE PIE
  1 batch of your favorite double crust
    pastry dough
  ½ cup sugar
  2 tablespoons tapioca or instant flour

⅛ teaspoon salt
½ teaspoon cinnamon
½ teaspoon ginger
¼ teaspoon nutmeg
3 tablespoons ginger marmalade
6 large tart apples, peeled, cored, sliced thin

1. Preheat oven to 415°F.

2. Line 9-inch pie plate with half the dough rolled to a circle about 11 inches

in diameter and ⅛-inch thick.

3. In large bowl, combine 6 dry ingredients and marmalade. Add apple slices and toss mixture until apples are well coated.

4. Turn mixture into pie plate.

5. Roll out remaining dough to a 12-inch circle ⅛-inch thick, then carefully lay over apple mixture. Seal and flute edges all around.

6. Make several slits in top to permit steam to escape.

7. Bake in 415°F oven 20 minutes, then reduce heat to 350°F and bake for 50 minutes.

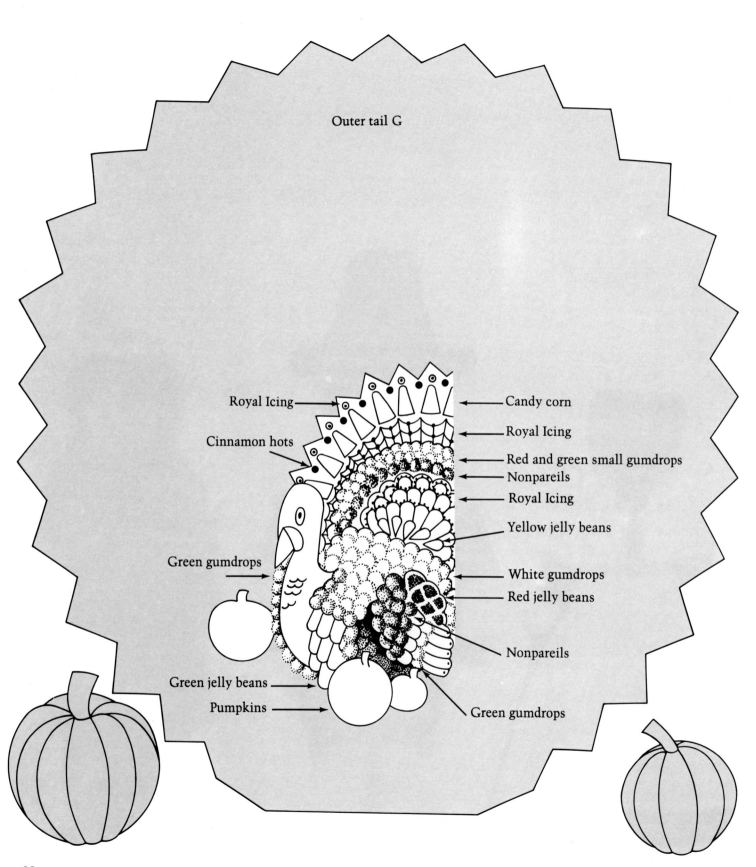

Outer tail G

Royal Icing

Cinnamon hots

Green gumdrops

Green jelly beans

Pumpkins

Candy corn

Royal Icing

Red and green small gumdrops

Nonpareils

Royal Icing

Yellow jelly beans

White gumdrops

Red jelly beans

Nonpareils

Green gumdrops

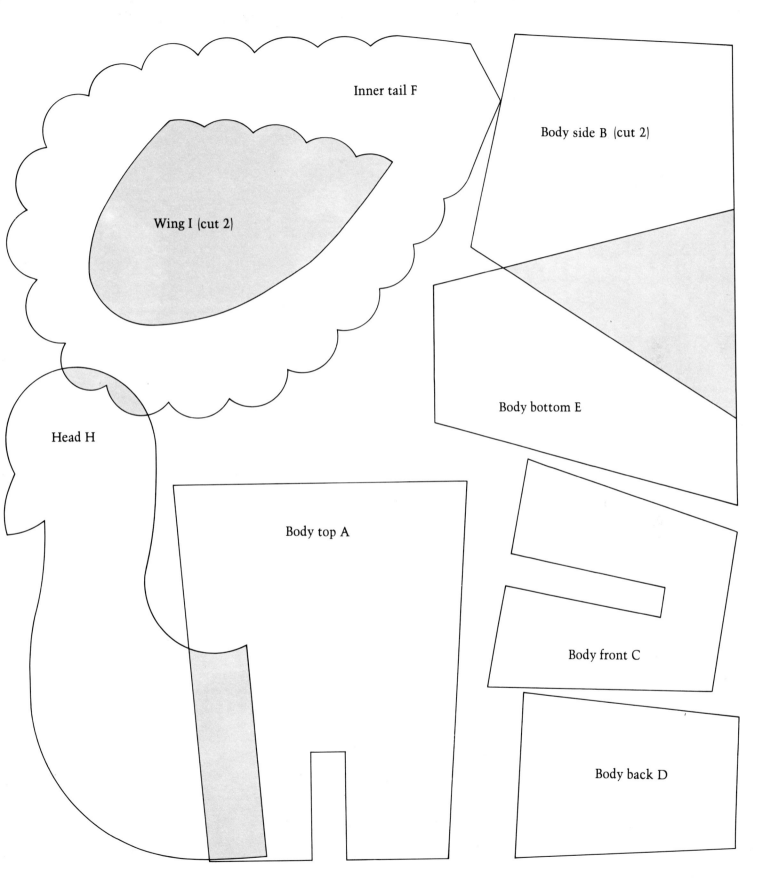

Inner tail F

Body side B (cut 2)

Wing I (cut 2)

Body bottom E

Head H

Body top A

Body front C

Body back D

Valentine Box

For a Valentine's Day mixer party, be as romantic as you've always wanted to be. Cover the table with your finest heirloom lace tablecloth, and add a silver candelabra or two flanking this wonderful gingerbread jewel box. Fill the box with heart-shaped cookies bearing romantic predictions:

A new person will enter your life.
An old friend will become
    a new love.
Trust your instincts.
Brown eyes are watching you.
A new job will bring a new love.
An invitation to lunch will provide
    new excitement.

You can easily turn heart-shaped cookies into "matchmaking fortune cookies" for a Valentine's Day mixer party. Make as many pink-trimmed cookies as there will be male guests and as many blue-trimmed ones as there will be female (or vice versa, if you must). Then, with red, pink, or silver ink, add the initials of an invited guest of the opposite sex and your prediction.

YOU WILL NEED:

1 batch Basic Molasses Gingerbread
  Dough
1 batch Royal Icing; Flow Frosting

MAKING THE PATTERNS

1. For both large- and medium-sized hearts, make tracing paper and cardboard patterns following instructions in Basic Skills chapter.
2. Make cookie pattern from small heart shape within medium heart.

MIXING THE DOUGH

Prepare 1 batch Basic Molasses Gingerbread Dough following recipe in Basic Skills chapter. Refrigerate at least 1 hour before rolling out.

CUTTING AND BAKING

1. Roll out dough and cut out box pieces on large foil-covered cookie sheet, following instructions in Basic Skills chapter.
2. Cut small heart out of medium heart, then transfer medium heart to a separate cookie sheet.
3. Place both sheets in 350°F oven.
4. Bake large heart pieces for 10 to 15 minutes or until edges have browned and pieces have set.
5. Bake medium heart for 5 minutes, then remove from oven and evenly sprinkle crushed cherry-colored hard candy into the center cut-out, making sure the edges are filled. Return to oven and bake about 7 to 10 minutes longer.
6. Cool pieces completely on rack before removing from cookie sheets and peeling off foil.
7. Roll, cut, and bake small heart cookies as directed above. Decorate to suit your own fancy.

ASSEMBLING AND DECORATING THE TOP

1. Prepare 1 batch Royal Icing, and mix some pink icing in a small bowl, following instructions in Basic Skills chapter.
2. Using metal spatula or kitchen knife, spread icing on underside of medium heart. Position in center of large heart and allow to set, about 5 minutes.
3. With small writing tip, pipe white "lace" around candy heart center of medium heart, and, before icing sets, position silver dragees.
4. Decorate rest of box top with white and pink icing, cinnamon hots, and silver dragees. Use color photograph and line art as guides, but let your own imagination work a bit as well. Allow top to dry completely, about 4 hours.

ASSEMBLING AND DECORATING THE SIDES

1. Using a #4 decorator's tip, pipe icing on bottom edge of 1 of 40 side pieces and position at a right angle along edge of box bottom. Hold until set.
2. Pipe icing along side and bottom of second side piece and position next to first. Repeat until all 40 side pieces are in place. Allow to dry completely.
3. Mix Flow Frosting, following instructions in Basic Skills chapter.
4. Spread white frosting around sides of box. When dry, apply final decorative touches with star and writing tips.

Pink icing ribbon

Cinnamon hots

Icing swirls

White icing "lace"

Silver dragees

Small heart for cookie

Medium heart for top center

Large heart for top and bottom (cut 2)

CHRISTMAS

CONTENTS

Grandma's House

Doesn't it look good? Think that icicle frosting dripping off the roof will last through the holidays? To divert nibblers from temptation, bake up a batch of house-shaped gingerbread cookies and decorate their roofs in the same way, with gobs of Royal Icing. Keep a dish of them nearby whenever little Miss Snitchy-Fingers comes around.

The patterns for grandma and the two children are made to scale, so the figures will fit on the porch or out front on the walk. Can't you almost smell the spicy fragrance of grandma's kitchen?

The construction of this house will be a challenge, even for an experienced gingerbread house contractor, because so many pieces— 45 in all—are used in the construction and decorative detail. And why not! After all, that is how the highly decorative style of Victorian architectural trim got its name.

YOU WILL NEED:

See Basic Skills chapter for equipment and materials you will need for making patterns, cutting out, baking, and decorating cookie pieces, and for propping structures while they dry.

In addition, have on hand full food cans.

1 batch Grandma's Gingerbread Dough
1 batch Royal Icing; Flow Frosting
2 pieces candy cane, each 3-inches long
1 piece red shoestring licorice, 2-inches long.

Candy for decorating: cinnamon hots, silver dragees, spearmint gumdrops.

A stiff, flat base of ¼-inch plywood or heavy cardboard, about 22 by 22 inches, on which to arrange the scene. Or, you can use a spare metal tray.

MAKING THE PATTERNS

The patterns for Grandma's House are ¼ size.

1. Enlarge patterns to full size following instructions in Basic Skills chapter.
2. Make and cut out cardboard patterns following instructions in Basic Skills chapter.

GRANDMA'S GINGERBREAD RECIPE

  9 cups unsifted flour
  ½ teaspoon salt
  2 cups dark corn syrup
1½ cups firmly packed dark brown sugar
1¼ cups margarine

1. In large bowl, combine flour and salt.
2. In 3-quart saucepan, combine corn syrup, brown sugar, and margarine. Cook over medium heat, stirring

constantly, until margarine is melted.
3. Stir into flour mixture until well blended.

CUTTING AND BAKING

Hint: you will be preparing and baking a total of 5 cookie sheets, but unless you have lots of them, you can prepare, bake, and cool 2 or 3 at a time. You can of course roll out all the dough to size on aluminum foil, then slide foil onto cardboard or large trays to refrigerate, and transfer to the cookie sheets after the first batch of dough is cooled and removed.

1. Line two or three 12 x 15½-inch cookie sheets with aluminum foil.
2. Place 2⅓ cups dough on each sheet and roll out to 11 x 15½-inch rectangles each ¼-inch thick.
3. Refrigerate 30 minutes.
4. Remove cookie sheets from refrigerator and cut out as many pattern pieces from each as you can, following instructions in Basic Skills chapter. Reserve excess dough.
5. Bake in 350°F oven 12 to 15 minutes or until cookie pieces are firm and lightly browned. Cool cookie sheets completely on racks before removing pieces from foil.
6. Continue cutting out and baking pieces until you have completed all of them.

DECORATING

1. Prepare 1 batch Royal Icing, divide into separate bowls, and tint to desired colors following instructions in Basic Skills chapter. Mix more Royal Icing as needed.

See Basic Skills chapter for instructions on applying Royal Icing and Flow Frosting.

2. Study the color photograph of Grandma's House. This is your guide for decorating the various pieces. You can duplicate our designs and color schemes, but do add your own personal touches too.
3. Begin decorating by piping white icing on pieces G, H, I, J, and K.
4. Pipe red icing to create shingle pattern on pieces L, M, and W. You may

want to color the sled red, too.

5. Pipe white icing to decorate pieces P and Q.

6. Pipe green icing to decorate pieces Y and Z.

7. Mix some Flow Frosting from the green icing and decorate both sides of all 4 tree pieces AA.

Hint: you may want to wait until tree is assembled before adding white icing "snow" to tips of tree branches.

8. Allow all decorated house pieces to dry completely (about 4 hours) before starting to assemble them.

Note: wait until after you have assembled the bay window to decorate pieces A, B, C, D, E, and F.

9. Decorate Grandma and the two children. You can use the full-color illustration as a guide for designs and colors, but give your own imagination a try too.

Note: as you assemble the parts of the house, hold pieces in place until set (about 5 minutes), before proceeding to the next step.

Remember "allow to dry completely" means you must let iced parts dry at least 4 hours before continuing assembly.

ASSEMBLING THE BAY WINDOW

1. Pipe white icing along bottom and side edges of bay-window front A and along the three shorter edges of bay-window bottom C. Place bottom of A on top front edge of C.

2. Pipe icing along bottom and 1 side of 1 piece bay-window side B and along bottom and opposite side of other piece B. Then place both Bs at sides of A and on top of C.

3. Pipe icing along top edges of A and both pieces B. Place bay-window top C on them.

4. Pipe icing along 3 shorter top edges of top piece C. Place bottom of bay-fence front D on top front edge of top piece C.

5. Pipe icing along bottom and 1 side of 1 bay-fence side E and along bottom and opposite side of other piece E.

Place each of pieces E at sides of D and on top of top piece C.

6. Pipe icing along outer edges of entire bay window. Position entire window on bay front F, 1 inch from the bottom and about ¾ inch from each side. Prop if desired and allow to dry completely.

7. Now decorate completed front bay section, piping white icing in designs to reinforce seams. Allow to dry completely.

ASSEMBLING THE HOUSE

1. Cut a stiff base of ¼-inch plywood or heavy cardboard that won't bend, or use a spare metal tray. The base should measure about 22 x 22 inches.

2. Starting with bay front F, pipe icing along bottom and right edge, then position on base.

3. Pipe icing along bottom and front edge of house side G, then place front edge of G on base and along right edge of F.

4. Pipe icing along bottom and left side of H where it joins G. Position on base and along back edge of G.

5. Pipe icing along bottom and edge of house side I where it joins H. Position on base and along edge of H.

6. Pipe icing along bottom and left edge of house-porch front J. Place on base and along front edge of I.

7. Pipe icing along bottom and both side edges of house-porch side K. Fit K into position on base and between side edges of J and F.

8. Using full food cans, prop house in position and allow to dry completely.

ATTACHING THE ROOF

1. Pipe icing along top edge of house back H and adjacent sloping edges of side pieces G and I. Position 1 piece house roof L on top. The roof will overhang slightly.

2. Pipe icing along top edge of other house roof L, along top edge of house-porch front J, and along front sloping edges of side pieces G and I. Position house roof L on top.

3. Pipe icing along top edge of left sloping side of bay front F, along top edge of house-porch side K, and along sloping side of 1 piece bay roof M.

Position M on top and against front house roof.

4. Pipe icing along top edge of right sloping side of bay front F, along top edge of house side G, and along sloping side edge and top edge of other piece bay roof M. Position M on top and against front house roof.

5. Pipe icing along 1 long edge of chimney side N. Position long edge of chimney front O along iced edge of N. Repeat with other chimney side and back.

6. Pipe icing along bottom edges of assembled chimney. Position in center of house roof top. Allow to dry completely.

7. Pipe icing along top sloping sides of gable P. Position under bay roof.

8. Pipe icing along angled bottom edge of 3 finials Q. Position on top of peaked roof edges. Allow to dry completely.

ASSEMBLING THE PORCH

1. Turn porch floor R decorated side down. Pipe icing along top edges of both porch-base sides S. Position 1 piece S on top of each short side edge of R.

2. Pipe icing along 1 long edge of porch-base front V and position along top front of porch floor R.

3. Turn assembled porch floor decorated side up.

4. Pipe icing on underside of short edges of step top T. Position across porch-base front V on step.

5. Pipe icing on undersides of short edges and along 1 long side of step front U. Position along front edge of step top T, connecting front edges of porch-base sides S. Allow to dry completely.

6. Pipe icing along bottom edges of assembled porch. Position porch on base against house-porch front J and house-porch side K.

7. Place porch roof W decorated side down. Pipe icing along sloping edge of porch-roof side X. Position X along underside of left side of porch roof W.

8. Cut 2 pieces of candy cane, each 3-inches long. Dot icing at 1 end of each piece. Position 1 cane at each front corner of porch floor.

9. Pipe icing along back edges and

right side edge of assembled roof. Dot icing on top of each candy cane. Position assembled roof against house-porch front J and house-porch side K so candy canes support front corners of assembled porch roof. Allow to dry completely.

ASSEMBLING THE CELLAR DOOR

1. Place cellar-door top Y decorated side down. Pipe icing along sloping edges of both cellar-door sides Z. Position them on top edges of long sides of cellar door top Y.

2. Pipe icing along bottom and back edges of assembled cellar door. Position against base of house side I. Allow to dry completely.

ASSEMBLING THE TREE

1. Pipe icing along straight edges of all 4 pieces AA, then fit them together at right angles. Hold in place 5 minutes, then allow to dry completely.

2. Pipe on white icing to frost tree branches.

ASSEMBLING THE SHOVEL

1. Cut small rectangle of leftover baked dough, measuring about ½ x ¾ inch.

2. Cut 1 piece red shoestring licorice 2 inches long. Pipe icing along licorice, then place on house-porch side K.

3. Pipe icing along ¾-inch side of shovel. Position shovel on porch floor R at an angle toward licorice handle. Allow to dry completely.

FINISHING TOUCHES

1. If desired, paint white Flow Frosting on roofs, porch, cellar door, and base to complete the snowy scene.

2. Pipe icing on spearmint gumdrops and position to make shrubbery.

3. Attach supports to grandmother and the 2 children with icing.

4. Arrange tree, sled, and grandma and the 2 children to complete the scene, applying icing if desired to secure figures.

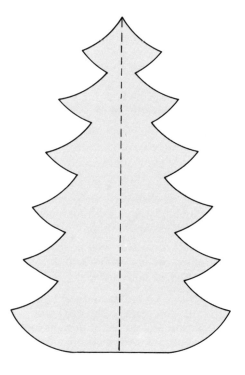

Tree AA

This is a full-sized pattern (cut 1, and ½)

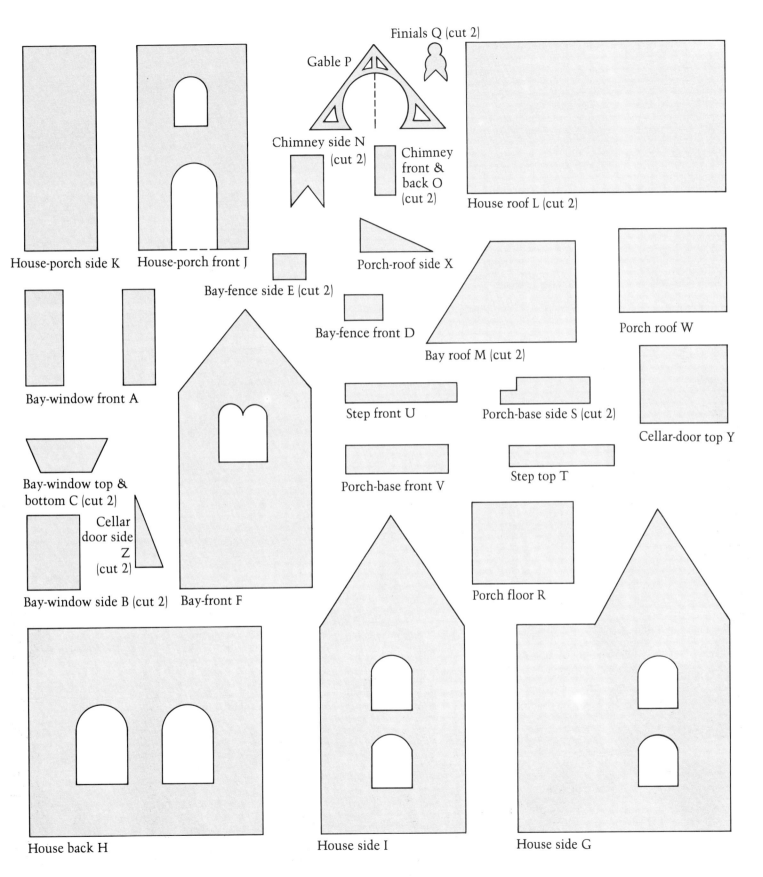

House-porch side K

House-porch front J

Finials Q (cut 2)

Gable P

Chimney side N (cut 2)

Chimney front & back O (cut 2)

House roof L (cut 2)

Porch-roof side X

Bay-fence side E (cut 2)

Bay-fence front D

Bay roof M (cut 2)

Porch roof W

Bay-window front A

Step front U

Porch-base side S (cut 2)

Cellar-door top Y

Bay-window top & bottom C (cut 2)

Cellar door side Z (cut 2)

Porch-base front V

Step top T

Bay-window side B (cut 2)

Bay-front F

Porch floor R

House back H

House side I

House side G

41

VICTORIAN CAROLERS

These gingerbread Carolers will cheerfully welcome the real carolers who come to your door, especially if both groups are surrounded by lots of good things to eat and drink. Also see the Recipes pages for other tempting hot grogs, cold punches, and, of course, the traditional eggnog.

These figures are easy to make and decorate because the full-sized patterns include details to mark on the dough before it is baked. This grouping, full-sized or reduced, will enliven your party centerpiece during the winter holidays. Such a scene might include the Village Church, the Colonial Saltbox, Grandma's House, or the Country Farm.

YOU WILL NEED:

See Basic Skills chapter for equipment and materials needed for baking and for decorating with Royal Icing.

A stiff, flat base, about 8½ x 14 inches, (optional) on which to arrange the figures, especially if the arrangement must be carried from place to place.

Shredded coconut for artificial snow (optional).

MAKING THE PATTERNS
Trace the full-sized patterns for the seven figures following instructions in Basic Skills chapter.

MIXING THE DOUGH
Spice Cookie Recipe
3½ cups unsifted flour
  1 teaspoon ground cinnamon
  ½ teaspoon ground nutmeg
  ½ teaspoon ground cloves
  ½ teaspoon ginger
  ⅛ teaspoon salt
  1 cup butter or margarine
  ⅓ cup firmly-packed light brown
    sugar
  ⅔ cup light corn syrup

1. In small bowl, stir together flour, spices, and salt.
2. In large bowl, using electric mixer at medium speed, beat butter or margarine until soft. Gradually beat in sugar. Beat in corn syrup until well blended. Reduce speed to low and gradually beat in flour mixture until well mixed.
3. Cover and refrigerate for several hours.

CUTTING AND BAKING
1. Line two 12 x 15½-inch cookie sheets with aluminum foil.
2. Remove chilled dough from refrigerator and divide in half, placing one portion on each cookie sheet.
3. Roll each portion of dough into an 11 x 15-inch rectangle about ¼-inch thick.
4. Cover cookie sheets with waxed paper and chill for at least 30 minutes, then remove from refrigerator.
5. Cut out cookie pieces and mark design details on the figures with pinpricks following instructions in Basic Skills chapter.
6. Bake pieces at 400°F for 10 to 15 minutes, or until they are set and lightly browned. Allow them to cool completely before decorating or removing from foil.

DECORATING
Make 2 batches of Royal Icing and decorate the cookies following recipe and instructions in Basic Skills chapter.

Full-sized patterns

43

ATTACHING SUPPORTS

1. Narrower caroling figures need one support, but wider ones may need two. Using white Royal Icing, "glue" supports perpendicularly to the backs of the figures so that, viewed from bottom, the support and figure form a T. The wide end of the support should be at the bottom.

2. Hold each support in place until icing sets, about 5 minutes. Then let figures dry completely (about 4 hours) before standing them up.

ARRANGING THE SCENE

1. Cut a stiff base of wood or heavy cardboard that won't bend, or use a spare metal tray. The base should measure about 8½ x 14 inches.

2. Cover base with aluminum foil and spread white Flow Frosting over all to simulate snow, or make a rim of white icing around the edge if you plan to use shredded coconut for the snow.

3. Arrange carolers and trees on base. If necessary, fasten the supports for the figures to the base with additional white icing, holding each figure in desired position until set, about 5 minutes.

4. For an even more wintry look, sprinkle coconut over entire scene.

MULLED CIDER

4 cups cider or unsweetened apple
   juice
8 cloves
2 sticks cinnamon
   Pinch of sugar

Full-sized patterns

Gently boil all ingredients together for about 10 minutes, then strain and serve hot in warmed glasses or coffee mugs. Garnish with a green holly leaf if desired. For the hard liquor crowd, add a shot of rum.

SWEDISH GLOGG
   1 quart port
   1 quart claret (dry red Bordeaux)
10 cardamom seeds
12 cloves
   2 sticks cinnamon (or more, to taste)
      Peel from ½ orange
   ½ pound seedless raisins
   ½ pound sugar
   1 pint vodka (brandy or gin may be substituted)
   ½ pound blanched almonds (optional)

1. Combine port and claret in saucepan. Tie spices and orange peel in cheesecloth bag and add to wines. Boil slowly for 15 minutes.
2. Add raisins and boil 15 minutes longer.
3. Remove saucepan from heat, and add sugar and vodka. When sugar is completely dissolved, return mixture to low heat. Add blanched almonds if desired and serve warm.
Yield: twenty 4-ounce cups.

HOT-BUTTERED CAROLERS
   ½ cup butter
   2 cups brown sugar
      Pinch of salt
   3 sticks cinnamon
   6 whole cloves
   2 quarts hot water
      Rum: 2 cups medium-colored or 1 cup light and 1 cup dark
   1 cup heavy cream, whipped
   ½ teaspoon nutmeg

1. Melt butter in small saucepan.
2. In large pot, mix sugar, salt, and spices and add butter.
3. Warm mixture over very low heat and add rum.

4. Ladle into glasses or cups.
5. Top each serving with whipped cream dusted with nutmeg.
Yield: twelve 8-ounce glasses or 24 punch cups.

The Village Church

White Georgian churches, with their tall steeples, are still familiar landmarks in country villages of both the old and the new worlds. The distinctive architecture of their spires, and the toll of their bells floating above the trees that hide their town, serve to orient the people of each town to the place and the time in which they live. In this gingerbread church, even the stained glass windows are made of sugar, and the bells are a chocolate kiss.

This church is an architectural companion to the Saltbox House. Together they set the stage for a holiday panorama that might include a town green (known as a "common" in New England) with the Victorian Carolers standing in it, the Country Farm at one end, and Grandma's House at the other. For one person to take on all those projects would be too much, but gingerbread construction is fun to do with other people. Wouldn't such a country village scene be a nice project for a church or other community group to undertake?

YOU WILL NEED:
See Basic Skills chapter for general equipment and materials

1 batch Old Village Dough
1 batch Royal Icing; Flow Frosting
1 batch Tinted-glass candy

A base of ¼-inch plywood or heavy cardboard at least 12 x 18 inches. Or, you can use a spare tray.

In addition, have on hand:
2-inch round cookie cutter,
full food cans for propping

Edibles:
Foil-wrapped chocolate kiss
Silver dragees
Red licorice laces (a total of at least 9 feet)
Red-and-white striped peppermints
Spearmint leaves
Gumdrop for wreath
Shredded coconut
Gumdrops or jelly beans for pathway

MAKING THE PATTERNS
The patterns for The Village Church are shown in reduced dimensions.

1. Make tracing paper patterns of all church pieces, using the full-sized dimensions given for each piece.
2. Draw in the design details—doors and windows—enlarged proportionally.
3. Make duplicate cardboard patterns following instructions in Basic Skills chapter.

MIXING THE DOUGH
Old Village Dough

8 cups unsifted flour
2 teaspoons ground cinnamon
2 teaspoons ground ginger
½ teaspoon salt
1¾ cups dark corn syrup
1 cup firmly-packed light brown sugar
¾ cup margarine or butter

1. In large bowl, combine flour, cinnamon, ginger, and salt.
2. In 2-quart saucepan, combine corn syrup, brown sugar, and margarine over medium heat, stirring occasionally, until ingredients are well blended.
3. Stir corn syrup mixture into flour mixture until well blended.
4. Knead dough with your hands until it is smooth and even in color.
5. Divide dough into 4 equal parts and wrap each in plastic wrap until ready to roll out.

MAKING THE "TINTED-GLASS" CANDY

⅓ cup sugar
⅓ cup light corn syrup
4 containers of different food colorings

1. Place an 18 x 12-inch piece of aluminum foil on a heat-resistant surface. Have food colorings handy.
2. In small saucepan, combine sugar and corn syrup. Stirring constantly, bring to boil over medium heat. Cook at full rolling boil without stirring for 2 minutes, then reduce heat to very low.
3. Pour approximately ¼ of the hot syrup mixture onto the foil, then return remaining syrup to low heat.
4. Quickly add about 3 drops of 1 food coloring to syrup on foil and stir until color is blended.
5. Repeat with each of 3 remaining colors, using ¼ of hot syrup for each.
6. Let the 4 candy mixtures stand about 20 minutes or until completely cool.
7. Place each color candy in a separate plastic bag and seal, then use a hammer or mallet to finely crush them. Store in tightly-covered containers in cool place until ready to use.

CUTTING AND BAKING

Hint: you will be preparing a total of 4 cookie sheets, but in this project you can bake only 2 at a time, because the cooking times and procedures are different.

If you don't have 4 cookie sheets, you can roll out the remaining dough to size on pieces of aluminum foil, slide foil onto cardboard or large trays to refrigerate, and then transfer to cookie sheets after the first baking is done.

1. Place ¼ of the dough on each of 4 foil-lined cookie sheets or pieces of foil.
2. Using a lightly floured rolling pin, roll out dough on two of the sheets to two 14 x 10-inch rectangles ¼-inch in thickness. Roll out dough on other two sheets to 13 x 11-inch rectangles of the same thickness.
3. Refrigerate sheets of rolled-out dough at least 30 minutes.
4. Lightly dust all cardboard pattern pieces with flour.
5. On one 14 x 10-inch rectangle, arrange pattern pieces for 2 side walls, belfry base, and belfry sides.

On one 13 x 11-inch rectangle, arrange pattern pieces for 1 side of roof and back wall.

6. Using a sharp, pointed knife, cut out pieces following instructions in Basic Skills chapter. Cut out side wall windows, then, using a 2-inch round cookie cutter, cut out space for rose window in back wall.
7. Bake these 2 cookie sheets in 350°F oven for 10 minutes, then remove from oven and let cool for 2 minutes.
8. Fill in window spaces with thin, even layers of tinted-glass candy. Sprinkle colors on one at a time, and be careful not to get candy on surrounding dough.
9. Return both cookie sheets to oven and bake 5 to 9 minutes longer or until edges begin to brown and pieces are set. Cool completely before removing from foil.

Hint: if candy windows stick to foil, remove entire piece with surrounding foil still attached, then gently peel foil away from underside.

10. On remaining 14 x 10-inch rectangle, arrange pattern pieces for right and left door; 4 sides of spire and spire base; front, back, and 2 sides of watchtower; step; and front and back of belfry.

On remaining 13 x 11-inch rectangle, arrange pattern pieces for other roof piece and front wall. Cut out pieces as above.

11. Bake both cookie sheets at 350°F for 15 minutes or until edges begin to brown and pieces are set. Cool and remove from foil as above.

Note: the various parts of The Village Church are decorated as they are assembled.

ASSEMBLING THE WATCHTOWER, BELFRY, AND SPIRE

1. Make 1 batch of Royal Icing. See Basic Skills chapter for instructions on preparing and applying Royal Icing.
2. Cut four 2½-inch pieces of red licorice lace.
3. Pipe icing along side edge of 1 watchtower front J. Attach 1 watchtower side K at right angle and hold until set, about 5 minutes.
4. Pipe icing along other side of J and attach other side K. Hold until set.
5. Pipe icing along exposed side edges of 2 side pieces K and attach watchtower back J. Hold until set.
6. Before icing sets, position 1 piece licorice along each seam, then ice 1 peppermint to each side as shown in photograph. Let dry at least 4 hours.
7. Assemble the 4 belfry walls G and H in the same way as the watchtower.
8. Cut four more 2½-inch pieces licorice and position on belfry seams. Let dry completely.
9. Assemble the 4 spire sides E in same way as watchtower.
10. Cut four 6-inch pieces licorice and position on spire seams. Let dry completely.

ASSEMBLING THE CHURCH

1. Cover base with aluminum foil. In the center, mark a 6 x 9-inch rectangle to indicate the location of the church walls.

2. Cut four 4-inch pieces of licorice.
3. Pipe icing along 1 side edge and the bottom edge of 1 side wall B. Pipe icing along back of 1 side edge and the bottom edge of front wall D. Using the rectangle you marked on the base as a guide, position B and D, placing edge of B against inside edge of D.

For extra strength, pipe additional icing along inside seam. Fill in any outside seam irregularities with icing, then, before icing dries, position 1 piece licorice on seam. Let icing set.

4. On other side wall B, pipe icing along bottom edge and the side edge that will form a corner with D. Pipe icing along inside of edge of D. Following markings on base, attach B to D. Reinforce seam if necessary and position 1 piece licorice on seam. Let icing set.
5. Pipe icing along bottom and inside edges of back wall C. Pipe icing along exposed edges of standing side walls and attach C to sides.

Reinforce inside seams with additional icing, then position licorice laces on both seams.

6. Pipe icing along top edge of 1 side wall B and nearest sloping edges of D and C. Pipe icing on underside of 1 roof piece A where it will rest on walls. Position A against iced edges of walls and hold until set.
7. To attach other roof piece, pipe icing in same way as for first piece, as well as along peak where 2 roof pieces will meet. Position other roof piece and pipe additional icing to fill in any spaces along peak. Prop if necessary, then let dry completely.

ASSEMBLING AND ATTACHING THE STEEPLE

1. Cut four 1½-inch pieces, four 1¾-inch pieces, eight 2-inch pieces, and four 2½-inch pieces of licorice lace.
2. Pipe icing along bottom edges of assembled watchtower and place in position on peak of roof.

Reinforce inside seams with more icing, then ice the four 1¾-inch licorice

pieces along seams as shown in photograph. Let icing set.

3. Pipe icing along top edges of assembled belfry and place base F on top. To represent bell, ice a foil-wrapped chocolate kiss to bottom of F so it is visible in arch of belfry. Ice four of the 2-inch licorice pieces horizontally beneath base F to cover seams. Let icing set.
4. Pipe icing along bottom edges of assembled belfry and place on belfry base I. Ice one 2-inch licorice piece along each seam joining belfry and I. Let icing set.
5. Pipe icing along top edges of watchtower and position assembled belfry. Ice the four 2½-inch licorice pieces to seams joining belfry and watchtower. Let icing set.
6. Pipe icing along bottom edges of assembled spire and place on spire base. Ice the four 1½-inch licorice pieces to seams. Allow entire structure to dry completely.

FINISHING TOUCHES

1. Decorate doors L and M, using icing to attach silver dragees and referring to the photograph as a guide. Let dry completely.
2. Pipe icing on underside of step N and position on base at front door opening.
3. Pipe icing along hinge sides of door pieces L and M and position on church front with doors slightly ajar.
4. Cut 2 pieces licorice the length of hinge sides of doors and ice to seams.
5. Ice gumdrop wreath above door.
6. Finish decorating The Village Church with assorted candies. You can use the photograph as your guide, or let your imagination run free.
7. Mix some Flow Frosting out of Royal Icing and spread entire base with it. See Basic Skills chapter for instructions on making and applying Flow Frosting. Before frosting dries, sprinkle base with shredded coconut, position spearmint leaf "bushes," and cut gumdrops or jelly beans in half to make a stepping stone pathway to the church doors. Allow Village Church to dry completely before moving it.

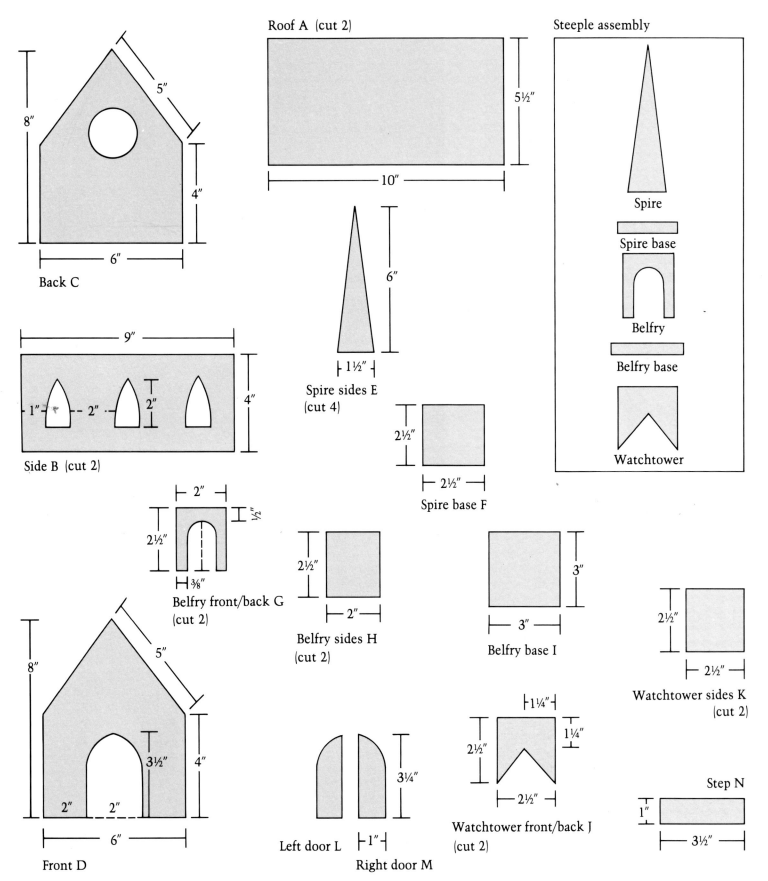

Back C

Roof A (cut 2)

5½"

10"

Steeple assembly

Spire

Spire base

Belfry

Belfry base

Watchtower

8"

5"

4"

6"

Side B (cut 2)

9"

1" 2" 2"

4"

Spire sides E
(cut 4)

6"

1½"

Spire base F

2½"

2½"

Belfry front/back G
(cut 2)

2"

½"

2½"

⅜"

Belfry sides H
(cut 2)

2½"

2"

Belfry base I

3"

3"

Watchtower sides K
(cut 2)

2½"

2½"

Front D

8"

5"

4"

3½"

2" 2"

6"

Left door L

Right door M

1"

3¼"

Watchtower front/back J
(cut 2)

1¼"

1¼"

2½"

2½"

Step N

1"

3½"

49

Saltbox House

The saltbox house is a New England tradition—and so is gingerbread. (It was an essential part of the Muster Day menu in colonial days and was included among the provisions to feed hungry sailors during the long voyages out of Boston or New Bedford.) Here, combining the two traditions, is a gingerbread saltbox that looks as if it had just been transplanted from the shores of Cape Cod. This project is a simple one, and good for beginners, including older children.

As you decorate the saltbox—or any other gingerbread project—take heart. Even experts sometimes make mistakes. If you examine the photo carefully, you'll see that the designer had to scrape off some of the icing around the door. You might not notice unless someone pointed it out, so don't think that a slip of the hand will ruin your work (even if faint traces of your repair work remain visible).

YOU WILL NEED:
See Basic Skills chapter for general equipment and materials.

1 batch gingerbread dough
1 batch Royal Icing
Red and green food coloring

In addition, have on hand: very large mixing bowl

A stiff base of ¼-inch plywood or heavy cardboard that won't bend, at least 10½ x 7½ inches. Or, use a spare metal tray or wooden cutting board as shown in photo.

MAKING THE PATTERNS
The patterns for the Saltbox House are shown in reduced dimensions. To make full-sized patterns, use ruler.

1. Make tracing paper patterns of wall, roof, and chimney pieces, using the full-sized dimensions given for each piece.
2. Draw in all the design details, enlarged proportionally—a scant 2½ times. The windows on your Saltbox House, for example, will be about 2-inches wide, including shutters, by 2-inches deep, including lintel and sill.
3. Make duplicate cardboard patterns following instructions in Basic Skills chapter.

MIXING THE DOUGH
This recipe makes enough dough for 2 of each pattern piece. After baking, select the better ones to use in assembling your house. You want to have "picture-perfect" pieces because this gingerbread construction is not painted with Flow Frosting. The surface of the house should be uniformly smooth, even, and consistent in texture. Use the extra pieces to make the front steps, and for snacking.

2 cups packed brown sugar
⅔ cup shortening
3 cups dark molasses
1⅓ cups cold water
14 cups all-purpose flour
4 teaspoons baking soda
2 teaspoons salt
4 teaspoons ginger
2 teaspoons ground cloves
2 teaspoons cinnamon

In a very large bowl, mix together brown sugar, shortening, and molasses until well blended, then stir in remaining ingredients. Cover and refrigerate a minimum of 4 hours.

CUTTING AND BAKING
1. Pinch off ¼ of the dough, return the rest to the refrigerator, and roll out dough on a lightly floured work surface to 1/16-inch thickness.
2. Roll dough around the rolling pin and carefully transfer to a large, lightly greased cookie sheet.

Note: you will roll, cut out, and bake 4 cookie sheets of dough altogether.

3. Lay out as many lightly floured cardboard pattern pieces as will fit easily on rolled-out dough, leaving at least ½ inch between each piece.
4. Cut around the outline of each pattern piece with a small, sharp knife. Remove scrap dough, roll again, and cut out front step pieces. Chill remainder of dough and make cookies later.
5. Place tracing paper pattern on top of each shape and mark design details by making pinholes through pattern into dough. See Basic Skills chapter for instructions on how to do this.
6. Bake at 375°F until no indentation remains when dough is pressed with the finger, about 10 minutes for larger pieces, 5 to 6 minutes for smaller ones.
7. Place cookie sheet on a rack to cool.
8. As first pieces are cooling, prepare second cookie sheet and continue rolling out, cutting, and baking until you have made 2 each of all pattern pieces. Cool all pieces completely before decorating.
9. Select the better pieces to decorate and use to construct the house.

DECORATING
1. Prepare 1 batch Royal Icing following recipe in Basic Skills chapter.
2. Spoon ⅓ cup icing into pastry bag or parchment cone fitted with #3 decorator's tip. See Basic Skills chapter for instructions on applying Royal Icing.
3. Following pinpricks in baked pieces, pipe design details on doors, windows, shutters, stonework, roof, and chimney.

Keep icing covered as you work so it doesn't dry out.

ASSEMBLING THE HOUSE
1. Assemble walls and roof of Saltbox House following instructions in Basic Skills chapter. Use white Royal Icing to join pieces.
2. To make chimney, pipe white icing on side edges of the 2 notched chimney pieces. Then press front and back chimney pieces into icing to form a box. Hold in place until set, about 5 minutes, then let dry completely (about 4 hours).
3. Pipe icing on bottom edges of chimney and position on roof.
4. Reinforce seams with more icing if necessary. Allow house to dry completely.
5. Cover plywood or cardboard base with aluminum foil, then pipe icing along all 4 edges of base and secure Saltbox to it.

FINISHING TOUCHES
1. In 2 small bowls, mix some red and some green Royal Icing. See Basic Skills chapter for instructions on tinting icing.
2. Pipe wreath and bow decorations on windows and doors. Allow to dry completely.

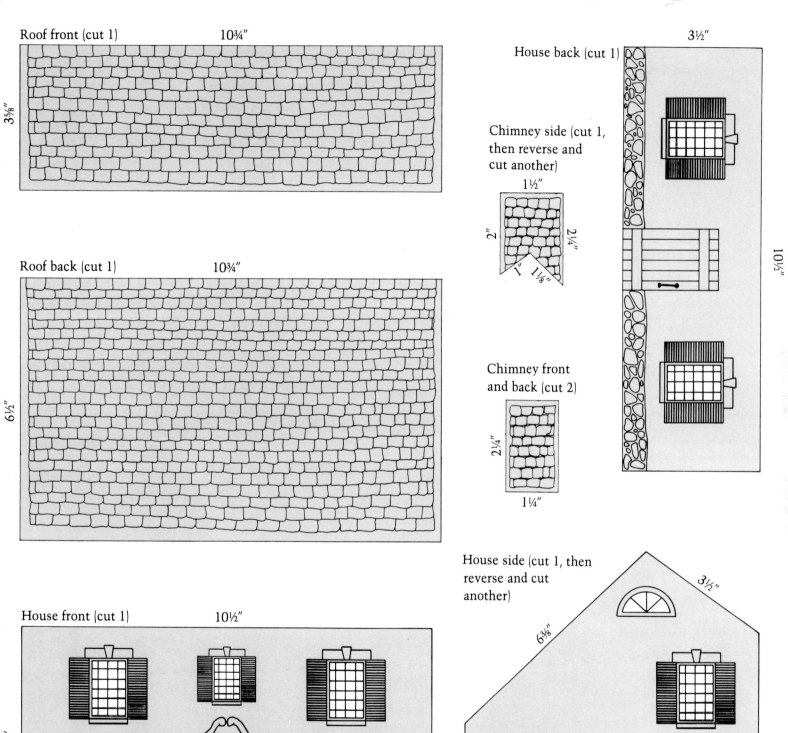

Roof front (cut 1) — 10¾"
3⅝"

House back (cut 1) — 3½"
10½"

Chimney side (cut 1, then reverse and cut another)
1½"
2"
2¼"
1" 1⅛"

Roof back (cut 1) — 10¾"
6½"

Chimney front and back (cut 2)
2¼"
1¼"

House front (cut 1) — 10½"
5¾"

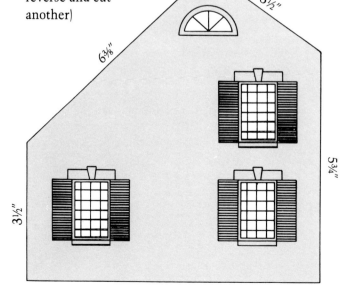

House side (cut 1, then reverse and cut another)
3½"
6⅜"
5¾"
3½"
7½"

CHildren's Village

This Christmas Village scene was made by four 7- to 12-year-olds. Each assembled and decorated a different building—large house, small house, church, and store. Because there is no baking, it's easy for young children to do. They can simply let their imaginations fly, decide what they want to make, assemble it, then decorate it to suit their fancies. Since this scene is constructed of commercial graham crackers in squares, rather than gingerbread, the kids can skip the tedium of mixing and baking. All they have to do is stick the crackers together with white (or colored) Royal Icing. It's as much fun as fingerpainting and building blocks combined (and you can eat the broken pieces).

YOU WILL NEED:

1 box graham crackers
1 batch Royal Icing; Flow Frosting Green, red, and black food colorings or whatever colors you want

In addition, from the kitchen cupboard have on hand: serrated knife for scoring crackers; small metal spatula; small plastic bowls; plastic wrap; small rubber spatula, knife, or paintbrushes; toothpicks

A sturdy base of ¼-inch plywood or heavy cardboard on which to arrange the buildings after they are all assembled and decorated. Or, borrow a large spare tray from your mother or father.

ASSEMBLING THE SMALL HOUSE

You need a batch of Royal Icing. You will use some of it to glue the pieces of the 4 buildings together. The rest you will color to decorate the buildings. Ask your mother or father, or an older sister or brother, to help make the icing, since the recipe calls for separating egg whites from yolks and for using an electric mixer. Instructions on making Royal Icing are in the Basic Skills chapter.

When the icing is made, leave half of it in the mixing bowl and put half of it in another bowl to use later. Cover both bowls tightly with plastic wrap. Keep them covered even while you are working with them or the icing will dry out.

1. Decide where you are going to work, then cover area with newspapers or an old cloth to protect it.
2. You will use 8 graham cracker squares to build the small house. Since the crackers come with 2 squares joined together, use a serrated knife to separate them. Carefully score each cracker, then break it gently along the scored line. Don't try to cut the cracker all the way through with the knife or it may shatter. Brush any crumbs off pieces.
3. Lay bottom cracker down flat. Use small metal spatula to spread white Royal Icing on 2 opposite edges of it.

Press 1 cracker side A on icing at a right angle to bottom cracker. Hold crackers in correct position for 3 minutes or until the icing is firm and the pieces stick together by themselves. Do the same for other side A. Don't worry if some of the icing squeezes out and shows.

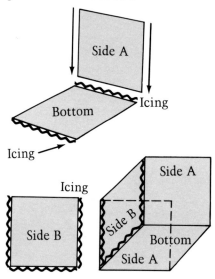

4. Spread icing on 3 edges of 1 side B. Press it along edge of bottom, between 2 side As. Hold until firm. Do the same for other side B. Now you have the house bottom and 4 walls. Make sure the house will stand alone before you start to put the roof on.

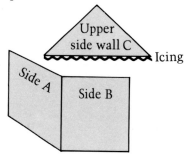

5. To make the upper side walls, put 1 cracker on cutting board and carefully score it from 1 corner to another with serrated knife, then break it apart. Now you have 2 triangles. Spread icing along bottom edge of 1 upper side wall C and put it on top of 1 side B. Hold until firm. Do the same for other upper side wall.

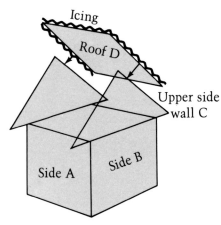

6. Spread icing on 3 sides of 1 roof D and press on slanted sides of 2 side wall Cs. Hold until firm, then do the same for other roof D. The roof will hang over the sides a bit.
7. Wait 15 minutes before starting to decorate the small house so icing can dry and all pieces are secured firmly in place.

DECORATING THE SMALL HOUSE

1. Decide how many colors you want to use, then have that many small plastic bowls ready. Put 2 tablespoons of Royal Icing in each bowl. See Basic Skills chapter for photographs and instructions on coloring icing using a toothpick and rubber spatula. Remember to keep the small bowls covered with plastic wrap at all times.

If you want to color a large area, thin some icing by stirring water into it a tablespoon at a time. This makes Flow Frosting.

2. Look at the pictures and read the instructions in Basic Skills chapter for applying Royal Icing and Flow Frosting. These will tell you how to use a pastry bag or parchment cone to apply icing and frosting. The pictures also show how to spread frosting with a spatula or knife, and how to paint it on with a brush.

3. Decide how you want to decorate the small house and dip into the icing and frosting! Apply 1 color at a time and let icing and frosting set for at least 5 minutes before adding more on top of 1 color or right next to it.

ASSEMBLING THE LARGE HOUSE, STORE, AND CHURCH

The other buildings basically are constructed in the same way as the small house.

1. To build the large house, leave 2 cracker squares joined for bottom, for front and back, and for roof pieces.

Attach the pieces in the same way and in the same order as you did for the small house. To make front steps, score and break some cracker squares into rectangular pieces and stack and ice them together. Hold until firm. Let house set for 15 minutes, then decorate as you wish.

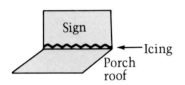
Sign
Icing
Porch roof

2. To build the store, follow instructions for the large house, but add a porch and a sign. Score and break 1 cracker square in half to make porch roof and sign. Spread icing along 1 long edge of a cracker half and place it at a right angle along the edge of the other half. Hold until firm.

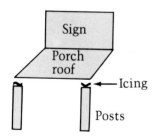
Sign
Porch roof
Icing
Posts

To make porch posts, score and break a cracker square to make 2 pieces each ½-inch wide. Spread icing along 1 short edge of each piece and place at right angles at corners of porch roof and sign piece.

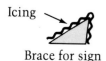
Icing
Brace for sign

Score and break 2 small triangles off 2 corners of a cracker square to make brace pieces to go between sign and store roof. To attach porch and sign, spread icing on 2 edges of each triangular piece and press straight side onto back of sign and angled side onto roof. Hold until firm. Let store set 15 minutes, then decorate as you wish.

3. To make rear roof, spread icing along all 4 edges of 1 cracker square and press on top of rear side walls and back. Hold until firm. Let church set 15 minutes, then decorate as you wish.

FINISHING TOUCHES

Someone in your house may be working on one of the other projects in this book right now. So have them roll, cut out, and bake gingerbread tree pieces for your village scene. See the tree pattern below.
When the tree pieces are baked and cooled completely, you can decorate and assemble them using icing to attach the 2 slotted parts.

To complete the Christmas Village scene, paint the base with poster paint or cover it with aluminum foil and spread white Flow Frosting all over the surface. Then arrange the 4 buildings and trees on it. If you wish, you can paint a backdrop for the scene.

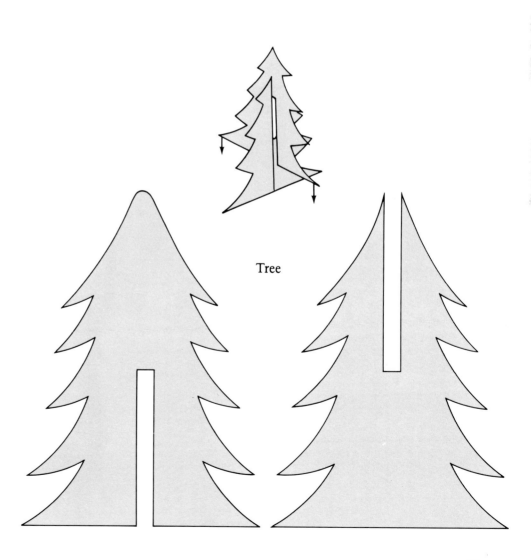
Tree

Window Trimmings

Of course, you painted the ornaments on *both* sides, so your guests (who are about to drive up the road to your house) and your neighbors can enjoy them from the outside too.

Hint: Whether you hang one or two in each pane as shown, make the loops of the bows separately (it's easier to get them all even that way). Push the tack up through the ribbon and bow-loops into the *underside* of the sash piece, not the front side. It looks better because the tack doesn't show or leave a hole that shows when you remove the tack after the holidays.

These charming ornaments look like gingerbread, but they're actually made from a durable, inedible dough that can be painted and sprayed with a clear sealer so they'll last for years. The Ginger Clay recipe given here, which can be cut in half, makes about 2 pounds of clay—that's enough for 10 to 15 ornaments, the largest of which is about 3½ x 6 inches.

To make window lites that will be slightly transparent if not painted, follow the recipe for Ginger Clay, but substitute 2 cups salt for the baking soda and decrease the water to 1⅓ cups. In a medium-sized saucepan, mix salt and ⅔ cup water. (Mixture will be thick.) Cook over medium heat, stirring occasionally, 5 minutes or until mixture begins to boil; remove from heat. Meanwhile measure cornstarch and mix with remaining ⅔ cup water. Stir all at once into salt and water mixture which has come to a boil. If mixture does not thicken, place over medium heat again and cook, stirring constantly, about 1 minute or until thickened. Turn out onto plate and cover with a damp cloth; cool. When cool enough to handle, knead thoroughly until smooth and pliable.

YOU WILL NEED:

See Basic Skills chapter for general material and equipment.

In addition, have on hand: ribbon, paper clips, waxed paper, sculpting tool or orange stick, paintbrush, acrylic paints, poster paints, or watercolors, quick-drying clear plastic spray, clear nail polish, or clear shellac.

MAKING THE PATTERNS

You can make your own patterns by tracing these full-sized pictures and following instructions in Basic Skills chapter, or you can use cookie cutters.

MAKING THE HANGERS

Straighten a paper clip, leaving a hook on each end. Cut the paper clip in half and you have two ready-made hangers.

MAKING THE GINGER CLAY

Make 1 batch

    1 cup cornstarch
    2 cups (1 pound) baking soda
    1 ½ cups cold water

1. In medium-sized saucepan, stir together cornstarch and baking soda.
2. Add water all at once and stir until smooth. Stirring constantly, cook over medium heat until mixture reaches consistency of *slightly* dry mashed potatoes. (Mixture will come to a boil, then start to thicken, first in lumps and then in a thick mass; it should hold its shape.)
3. Turn out onto plate, cover with damp cloth, and let cool.
4. When cool enough to handle, knead thoroughly on cornstarch-dusted surface until smooth and pliable.
5. If not to be used immediately, store completely cooled clay in tightly closed plastic bag or container with tight-fitting cover. Clay may be kept in cool place up to two weeks. Knead stored clay thoroughly before using.

MAKING THE ORNAMENTS

1. Working with a small amount of clay at a time, roll it out to ½-inch thickness on waxed paper or on a work surface lightly dusted with cornstarch.

Hint: To keep waxed paper from wrinkling, slightly moisten work surface before laying paper down. Keep remaining clay in tightly closed container.

2. Cut out ornament shapes following instructions in Basic Skills chapter or use cookie cutters.
3. Smooth and shape outer edges of each cookie using a sculpting tool or an orange stick from a manicure kit.
4. Press this same tool gently into clay to define certain lines, such as the snowman's legs; the gingerbread house windows, door, and lattice work; the stocking heel and toe.

If you wish, you can add three-dimensional hand-shaped details such as buttons, scarf, and bow-tie for the snowman; a toy bag for Santa Claus; trimming on the star and bell; buttons, scarf, and tassel on the gingerbread man's hat; the angel's book and hands; the reindeer's ear and harness; a base and garland on the Christmas tree.

Hint: to join pieces of clay or add one layer to another, moisten the area of contact on the ornament with a wet paintbrush, then gently press on the detail pieces.

5. Insert a hanger into top center of each ornament.
6. To dry ornaments, place finished pieces, decorated side up, on wire rack or protected surface. Clay will dry and harden at room temperature. When ornament fronts are dry to the touch (several hours or overnight), turn them over and continue drying, turning occasionally.

Hint: if small pieces should come off in drying, let dry completely then glue them back in place with white glue.

To speed-dry ornaments, preheat oven to 350°F. When this temperature is reached, turn oven off. Place clay ornaments on cooling rack or on waxed-paper-covered cookie sheet and put in oven. Let dry in oven until oven is cold, turning occasionally. If necessary, continue drying at room temperature, turning occasionally.

DECORATING

1. When ornaments are thoroughly dry, give them an overall coat of paint in a light brown (gingerbread) color using acrylic paints, poster paints, or watercolors. Let this coat dry thoroughly.
2. Paint over gingerbread color with whichever other colors you choose, following the defining lines and details you outlined earlier.
3. For a shiny finish and extra strength, spray completely dry, painted ornaments with 3 to 4 coats of quick-drying clear plastic spray. Allow ornaments to dry thoroughly between coats. Or, you can paint them with clear nail polish or dip them in clear shellac.

Left: *The stuffed bird, sharing a piece of gossip with the gingerbread bird, can't understand why he's not getting a reaction.* **Below:** *An Austrian ornament pressed from an antique mold bears the first three initials of the old Greek word for the name of Christ, "IHSOUS".*

ORNAMENTS

Above: *A gingerbread Chanticleer, (French Tirol) seeing the candle, thinks it's sunup, throws back his head and crows.* **Right:** *Traditional tree ornaments fashioned from gingerbread by a variety of American designers.*

In Austria, the Tirol especially, the figure of St. Nicholas is a squat, gnome-like presence when he makes an appearance during the holiday season as a homemade gingerbread figure. Sometimes, as shown in these photographs, he stands by in centerpieces to keep an eye on children's behavior; sometimes he hangs from the tree.

Every country that celebrates the Christmas season has some special kind of cookie recipe and design for that season. In Sweden, hearts are the special shape for Christmas. In the German-speaking countries, St. Nicholas. In English-speaking families, many shapes appear on the tree, among them stars, angels, Santas, sleighs. These pages and the one prior offer some ideas for homemade ginger-cookie ornaments for the tree; all of them demonstrate the creative spirit of joy and sharing.

Gift-Wrapped Goodies

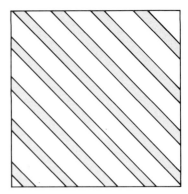

It may be that the toy kitten is the gift inside the gingerbread gift-wrapped box, or perhaps the kitten is waiting until someone can untie the little present for her. Meantime, she's climbed into the box because it smelled so good. Perhaps too, just a moment ago, someone tucked her new angora toy into the open box to keep it clean while she went to get a Christmas bow to tie around its neck.

This marvelous gift box is edible right down to the ribbon. The box stands about 6½-inches high and is 8½-inches square. The box and the top of the lid are decorated with stripes of white and colored Flow Frosting, and then wrapped with strips of plum, raspberry, or strawberry "leather" (fruit syrup baked in thin sheets). You can use the box as a party centerpiece—fill it with cookies, colorful hard candies, wrapped chocolates, candy canes, a low

vase of fresh flowers or, best of all, squares of warm, fragrant Gingerbread Cake to be served with pitchers of Custard or Lemon Sauce (see following recipes). Let the box dry completely for at least five days before putting anything steamy or moist inside it, or it may sag. Even when it is dry, line it with plastic wrap or waxed paper before putting flowers or fresh-baked goodies in it.

YOU WILL NEED:
See Basic Skills chapter for general equipment and materials

1 batch Basic Honey Gingerbread Dough
1 batch Royal Icing; Flow Frosting
1 batch Plum Leather (or 6 packages ready-made raspberry, strawberry, or plum fruit leather)

MAKING THE PATTERNS
Using ruler, draw and cut 3 cardboard patterns: an 8½-inch square for the top, an 8-inch square for the bottom, and a 6 x 8-inch rectangle for the sides.

MAKING THE DOUGH
Prepare 1 batch Basic Honey Gingerbread Dough following recipe in Basic Skills chapter.

Roll out, cut, and bake cookie pieces following instructions in Basic Skills chapter.

DECORATING
1. Make 1 batch of Royal Icing and mix some Flow Frosting, following instructions in Basic Skills chapter.
2. Paint diagonal stripes of white Flow Frosting on 1 side piece. See Basic Skills chapter for instructions on applying Flow Frosting. Paint stripes

from upper left-hand to lower right-hand corner. Paint all white stripes, let dry thoroughly (about 1 hour), then paint all green stripes. Repeat with second side piece.
3. Follow step 2 for other 2 side pieces, but paint white and green stripes from upper right-hand to lower left-hand corner.
4. Paint diagonal white and green stripes on top of box.

ASSEMBLING THE BOX
1. Using pastry bag with #4 metal tip, pipe small amount of Royal Icing along 6-inch edge of 1 side piece. Position second side piece at right angle to iced edge, making sure that stripes match. Hold in place until set, about 5 minutes.

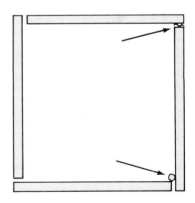

2. Ice and attach remaining sides following diagram.
3. Reinforce inside corners with extra icing and allow to dry thoroughly, about 4 hours.
4. Place small amount of icing on bottom edges of box and place on top of 8-inch square piece, then dry thoroughly.

5. Carefully fill in corners with green or white Flow Frosting wherever necessary to give the wrapped box a finished look then allow to dry completely.

ATTACHING THE RIBBON

1. Prepare or purchase fruit leather.
2. Cut fruit leather into 13 strips, each 1 x 6-inches long.
3. Pipe small amount of icing down the center of 1 strip and hold in a vertical position on the center of one side of box until set. Repeat for remaining 3 sides.

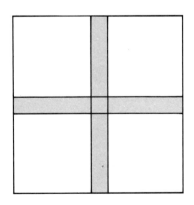

4. Pipe icing down the center of 4 more strips and arrange them on the box top following diagram, making sure they line up with the strips on the sides of box. Hold each in place until set.

MAKING THE BOW

1. Take 1 strip and loop the ends in toward the center. Use icing to secure ends in place, then hold in place until set. Do the same for 3 more strips.

2. Arrange strips in star fashion, then use icing to secure each loop to the one below it, holding each in place until set.

3. Loop remaining strip in a circle and secure ends with icing. When set, attach to center of overlapped strips and hold in place until set.

4. Attach bow to center of crossed strips on top of box with icing, then allow to dry completely.

Now your gift-wrapped box is ready to surprise someone and you probably want to put something inside it. If you plan to serve something warm in the box, such as Gingerbread Cake, make sure the box is thoroughly dry first—allow at least 5 days.

PLUM LEATHER

  2 pounds sweet red plums
  ½ cup light corn syrup

1. Preheat electric oven to warm (140 to 150°F. For gas ovens, the pilot light alone should provide enough warmth to maintain desired temperature.
2. Rinse, pit, and slice plums.
3. Place plums and corn syrup in 4-quart saucepan and bring to boil, stirring occasionally. Reduce heat and cook gently, uncovered, stirring occasionally, until plums are very soft.
4. Put mixture through food mill to puree.
5. Line two 10 ½ x 15 ½ x 1-inch baking pans with clear plastic wrap, letting it extend ¾-inch up the edges of the long sides of the pan. Allow enough extra plastic wrap to bring it over the shorter ends and secure to underside of pan with masking or scotch tape.
6. Pour equal amounts of plum puree into each lined pan, then, with rubber scraper or metal spatula, spread mixture thinly and evenly in each pan to within 1 inch of edge.
7. Place pans in middle of oven, leaving door slightly open. Periodically check oven thermometer temperature and adjust as necessary to maintain 140 to 150°F. Drying time will be about 24 hours. The plum puree will be dry enough when, after loosening an edge with a small spatula, it can be peeled away from the plastic wrap in a sheet.
8. Remove plum leather from original plastic wrap and place it on a clean piece of plastic wrap several inches longer than the leather.
9. Roll the leather jelly-roll fashion from the narrow edge so plastic wrap touches each part, then seal ends with plastic ties or small rubber bands. Store in refrigerator up to 3 months or in freezer up to 6 months.
Yield: 2 rolls.

PARTIES

CONTENTS

The firemen have rushed off to fight the fire, leaving their checker game unfinished. The chief is just as glad—he's losing. Perhaps that's why he has taken a bite out of one of the pieces. Even in a gingerbread world, the guys in the white hats don't always win!

Tension is mounting; time has almost run out for this move. These International Grand Masters were supposed to be evenly matched. Could one of them have threatened a massive, retaliatory munch!

GAMES

Gingerbread adds a new element of suspense to three classic games: chess, checkers, and Chinese checkers. Will the players make it through the game without eating the pieces? Or will they go Jump (munch) Jump (munch) across the board? Better bake up a big batch of extra pieces just to be safe.

Even the boards are gingerbread. Use the same board for both chess and checkers. The chessmen are decorated with white frosting; the checkers with red and green candied cherries. And— get this—the "marbles" for Chinese checkers are *chocolate truffles*. You could substitute colored gumdrop marbles, of course, but victory wouldn't be half as sweet.

Using chopsticks to play Chinese checkers may slow down your game, but it will also keep your weight down. The delicious irony in using chocolate ffles for marbles lies in the moral "To the victor belong the calories."

FOR THE CHESS/ CHECKERBOARD, 48 CHECKERS, AND 32 CHESSMEN YOU WILL NEED:

See Basic Skills chapter for general equipment and materials.

1 batch Light Gingerbread Dough
1 batch Dark Gingerbread Dough
1 batch Royal Icing; Flow Frosting

6 red and 6 green candied cherries, cut in halves, for checkers

In addition, have on hand:
1 ¼-inch cookie cutter for checkers and for stands for chessmen

MAKING THE CHESS/ CHECKERBOARD PATTERNS

1. Draw and cut out one 13-inch square and one 12-inch square from tracing paper.
2. Measure and draw lines dividing the 12-inch square into 8 strips 1½-inches wide and 12 inches long.
3. Repeat crosswise to make 64 1½-inch squares.

MIXING THE DOUGH

Light Gingerbread Dough

3½ cups all-purpose flour
  1 tablespoon ground ginger
  ⅓ cup granulated sugar
  ⅛ teaspoon salt
  ⅔ cup light corn syrup
  1 cup butter, melted

Dark Gingerbread Dough

3½ cups all-purpose flour
  1 teaspoon cinnamon
  ½ teaspoon ground cloves
  2 teaspoons ginger
  ⅓ cup dark brown sugar
  ⅛ teaspoon salt
  ⅔ cup light molasses or dark corn syrup
  1 cup butter, melted

1. Combine dry ingredients in large bowl.
2. Make a well in center of dry ingredients and add corn syrup or molasses, then butter. Stir with fork until mixture is well blended.

3. Wrap dough in plastic wrap and set aside until you are ready to roll it out, but no longer than 1 hour.

CUTTING AND BAKING THE CHESS/CHECKERBOARD

1. Prepare 1 batch of each dough recipe.
2. Line a cookie sheet at least 14 x 16 inches with lightly oiled foil.
3. Flour rolling pin and roll out half of Dark Gingerbread Dough on cookie sheet to ³⁄₁₆-inch thickness to make a square slightly larger than 13 inches. Chill 30 minutes in refrigerator or 10 minutes in freezer.
4. Roll out half of Light Gingerbread Dough on piece of lightly oiled foil to ³⁄₁₆-inch thickness to make a rectangle slightly larger than 12 x 6 inches and chill as above.
5. Lightly flour 13-inch square pattern and place it on dark dough. Trim around edges with sharp, pointed knife, then remove pattern.
6. Lightly flour 12-inch square pattern and center it on 13-inch square of dark dough. Score around pattern with knife, cutting about half-way through dough. Then with 12-inch pattern still in place, draw over lines with knife just firmly enough to mark 64 1½-inch squares on dough, then remove pattern.
7. Starting at edge nearest you, carefully cut around and remove every other square of dough in first row, leaving border intact. In second row, cut around and remove squares above remaining dark squares in first row. Repeat to make the 64-square checkerboard pattern.
8. Cut 12-inch square pattern in half to make a 12 x 6-inch rectangle, then flour lightly and place on Light Gingerbread Dough. Trim edges around pattern with knife, then draw over squares, pressing just hard enough to mark 32 1½-inch squares on dough. Remove pattern.
9. Cut all the way through dough with knife to separate the squares, then carefully fit light dough squares into open spaces in checkerboard.
10. Bake at 350°F until checkerboard feels firm and light dough is golden— about 10 minutes.

11. Cool on cookie sheet 10 minutes, then carefully remove checkerboard, still on foil, to a rack and cool completely.

ATTACHING THE CHESS/CHECKERBOARD BASE

1. Prepare 1 batch Royal Icing following instructions in Basic Skills chapter.
2. Cut out a 13-inch square of cardboard.
3. Place cookie sheet over checkerboard and gently turn both over, then carefully peel foil off underside of baked board.
4. Ice cardboard lightly, using a small spatula or kitchen knife, then fit cardboard, iced side down, onto back of board.
5. Now turn board right side up, using the cookie sheet for support.
6. Remove cookie sheet and allow board to dry for several hours. Dry overnight before using it.

CUTTING AND BAKING THE CHECKERS

1. Roll out remaining light dough to ³⁄₁₆-inch thickness on lightly oiled foil, then chill 30 minutes in refrigerator or 10 minutes in freezer.
2. Cut out 24 rounds of dough using a 1 ¼-inch round cookie cutter.
3. Carefully place checkers on lightly oiled cookie sheet about 1 inch apart.
4. Roll out remaining dark dough to ³⁄₁₆-inch thickness, chill, cut, and place on second cookie sheet as above to make 24 more checkers.
5. Bake checkers at 350°F about 8 minutes. Cool completely.

DECORATING THE CHECKERS

1. Attach a star tip to a pastry bag or parchment cone, then fill with Royal Icing, following instructions in Basic Skills chapter.
2. Pipe icing stars in the center of 12 light and 12 dark checkers, following instructions in Basic Skills chapter for applying icing.
3. Cut 6 red and 6 green cherries in half, then press red cherries into icing on light checkers and green cherries into icing on dark checkers. Allow to

dry completely, about 1 hour. Use remaining checkers for making kings.

CUTTING AND BAKING THE CHESSMEN

1. Prepare patterns, following instructions in Basic Skills chapter.
2. Roll out remaining light dough to ³⁄₁₆-inch thickness on lightly oiled foil, then chill 30 minutes in refrigerator or 10 minutes in freezer.
3. Place patterns on dough and cut around them with a sharp knife. Make 2 rooks, 2 knights, 2 bishops, and 8 pawns.
4. Using the pattern markings as your guide, score design details on chess pieces.
5. Carefully place chessmen 1 inch apart on lightly oiled cookie sheet.
6. Knead together scraps of light dough, then roll out to ³⁄₁₆-inch thickness and cut 16 rounds using a 1¼-inch round cookie cutter. Rounds will be the stands for the pieces.
7. Place rounds on lightly greased cookie sheet.
8. Bake light chess pieces and rounds at 350°F until golden—about 8 minutes.
9. Roll out remaining dark dough, chill, cut, score, and bake as above to make chess pieces and rounds for bases.

DECORATING THE CHESSMEN

1. Attach a writing tip with adapter to a pastry bag or parchment cone, then fill with white Royal Icing, following instructions in Basic Skills chapter.
2. Decorate chess pieces with icing, using your score marks and the color photograph as your guides, and following instructions in Basic Skills chapter for applying icing.
3. Let pieces dry at least ½ hour.

ATTACHING THE CHESSMEN'S STANDS

1. Attach star tip to pastry bag, then fill with white Royal Icing.
2. Pipe icing stars in center of 16 light and 16 dark cookie rounds, following instructions in Basic Skills chapter.
3. Press each chessman into icing in the center of a round and hold long enough for it to stay upright by itself.

These are full-sized patterns.

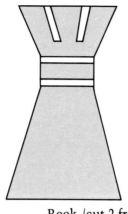

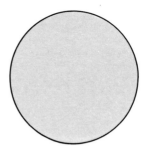

Stand (cut 16 from each batch)

Rook (cut 2 from each batch)

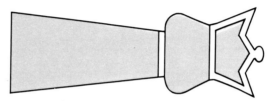

Queen (cut 1 from each batch)

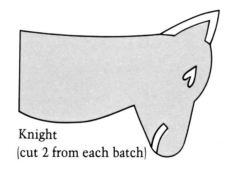

Knight (cut 2 from each batch)

Pawn (cut 8 from each batch)

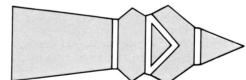

Bishop (cut 2 from each batch)

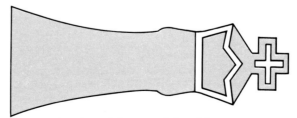

King (cut 1 from each batch)

FOR THE CHINESE CHECKERBOARD YOU WILL NEED:

See Basic Skills chapter for general equipment and materials.

1 batch Light Gingerbread Dough
1 batch Dark Gingerbread Dough
1 batch Royal Icing; Flow Frosting

    Food coloring: red, yellow, blue, green, orange
1 batch Chocolate Truffles or 60 colored gumdrops

In addition, have on hand:
Compass or 14-inch round tray or plate, piece of cardboard at least 14 inches square, 6 small bowls.

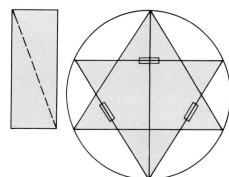

MAKING THE CHINESE CHECKERBOARD PATTERNS

1. Draw and cut out a 14-inch circle from tracing paper using a compass or a large tray or plate as your guide.
2. Draw and cut out a 12 x 10½-inch rectangle from tracing paper.
3. Fold rectangle in half to make a 10½ x 6-inch rectangle, then draw a diagonal line from 1 corner to the opposite corner. Cut along the line.
4. Open pattern and make another one identical to it. On each triangle, draw a center line from any angle to the center of the opposite side.
5. Place circle pattern on table and lay 1 triangle on top of it so the 3 points all touch the edges of the circle.
6. Place other triangle on top turned in the opposite way, with center lines going in the same direction. Its 3 points should also touch the edges of the circle. Tape the 2 triangles together to make a 6-pointed star.

CUTTING AND BAKING THE CHINESE CHECKERBOARD

1. Prepare 1 batch Dark and 1 batch Light Dough, following the recipe at the beginning of this chapter.
2. Line a cookie sheet at least 15 x 17 inches with lightly oiled foil.
3. Flour rolling pin and roll out dark dough on cookie sheet to make a circle slightly larger than 14 inches, then place circle pattern on dough and trim edges with a sharp, pointed knife. Chill 30 minutes in refrigerator or 10 minutes in freezer.
4. Roll out light dough on lightly oiled foil to make a 14-inch or slightly larger circle, then place star pattern on light dough and cut out with a knife. Chill as above.
5. Place star pattern on dark dough circle, carefully cut around it with knife, and remove dark star.
6. Carefully peel foil from back of light dough star and fit it into space where dark star was removed.
7. Dip the tip of the handle of a wooden or plastic spoon in flour and, starting with the point of the star nearest you, press an indentation into the light dough near the tip of one point of the star. Make rows of 2, 3, and, at the widest part of the point, 4 indentations. Repeat on other points of star. Use the color photograph as your guide.
8. Now make rows of indentations in the center of the star.
9. Bake at 350°F until board feels firm to the touch and light dough is golden—about 10 minutes.
10. Cool 10 minutes on cookie sheet, then carefully remove checkerboard, still on foil, to a rack and cool completely.

You may jump over an occupied spot into an empty one and take the piece you jumped.

ATTACHING THE CHINESE CHECKERBOARD BASE

1. Prepare 1 batch Royal Icing following instructions in Basic Skills chapter, but when mixture is well combined but still quite thin, spoon out 2 tablespoons into each of 6 small bowls and cover each tightly with plastic wrap. This is Flow Frosting, and you will use it later to decorate the board.

2. Cut out a 14-inch circle of cardboard.

3. Place cookie sheet over checkerboard and gently turn both over. Carefully peel foil off underside of baked board.

4. Ice cardboard lightly, using a small spatula or kitchen knife. Then fit cardboard, iced side down, onto back of board.

5. Now turn board right side up, using the cookie sheet for support. Remove the cookie sheet and allow board to dry several hours. Dry overnight before using it.

DECORATING THE CHINESE CHECKERBOARD

1. One at a time, uncover 5 of the 6 bowls of Flow Frosting and add food coloring to achieve the desired tints of red, yellow, blue, green, and orange. Cover each bowl again immediately after mixing in food coloring. Follow instructions in Basic Skills chapter for tinting Flow Frosting using a toothpick and spatula.

2. Paint each point of the star with a different color, following the instructions in the Basic Skills chapter for applying Flow Frosting.

3. Let star dry until frosting is hard, about 1 hour, but dry longer before using board.

MAKING THE MARBLES

Prepare 1 batch of Chocolate Truffles according to the following recipe, or use gumdrops of 6 different colors.

Chocolate Truffles

    2 boxes (2½ ounces each) snack-size chocolate wafers

    1 bar (4 ounces) sweet cooking chocolate

    1 tablespoon brandy or liqueur or ½ teaspoon vanilla extract

    ⅓ cup light corn syrup

For decorating: Light corn syrup, finely chopped nuts, finely chopped coconut, colored candy shot, chocolate sprinkles, unsweetened cocoa, confectioner's sugar

1. Roll cookies into crumbs with rolling pin or grind in food processor with chopping blade.

2. Melt chocolate over hot, not boiling, water. In medium bowl, combine cookie crumbs, melted chocolate, brandy, and corn syrup. Stir until well blended.

3. Take generous ¼ teaspoon of chocolate mixture and roll into a "marble" slightly less than ½-inch in diameter. You should be able to make about 80 marbles.

4. Dip 40 marbles in corn syrup, and roll 10 in chopped nuts, 10 in coconut, 10 in candy shot, and 10 in chocolate sprinkles.

5. Without dipping in corn syrup, roll 10 in cocoa and 10 in confectioner's sugar.

6. Roll remaining marbles in leftover coatings and serve as snacks.

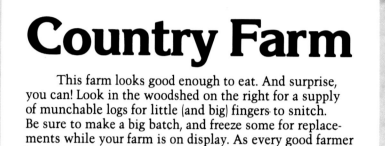

Country Farm

This farm looks good enough to eat. And surprise, you can! Look in the woodshed on the right for a supply of munchable logs for little (and big) fingers to snitch. Be sure to make a big batch, and freeze some for replacements while your farm is on display. As every good farmer knows, there's nothing worse than an empty woodshed.

This country farm nestles snugly in soft, snow-covered hills. To duplicate this winter barnyard scene, arrange some pillows on a table to create the "hills", then completely cover the pillows and table with a large, light-colored blanket. Sprinkle the hills with artificial snow and arrange the farm and animal pieces. Sprinkle some more snow around the barn and the figures. To create a warm-weather farm scene, eliminate the artificial snow (white icing) on the barn, and the sleigh and wreath pieces. Replace the holly design over the door with a hex sign and change the icing color for the base.

YOU WILL NEED:

See Basic Skills chapter for general equipment and materials.

3 batches gingerbread dough
3 batches Royal Icing; Flow Frosting

A 20 x 24-inch base of ¼-inch plywood or other stiff material.

MAKING THE PATTERNS

1. For barn and woodshed: following the dimensions provided, use ruler to transfer patterns onto lightweight cardboard. Be sure to draw all windows, doors, and circles for placement of hex signs onto patterns, but do not cut them out. Cut openings for barn doors, woodshed door, and second-story barn window *only*.
2. Make a paper tracing of barn and woodshed patterns.
3. Full-sized patterns are provided for animals, trees, farmer, sleigh, wreath and hex signs. Copy these designs from the book onto tracing paper, then transfer them to cardboard and cut them out.

MIXING THE DOUGH

Make 3 separate batches. Do not triple.

   3½ cups unsifted flour
    2 teaspoons ground cinnamon
    ½ teaspoon ground nutmeg
    ½ teaspoon ground cloves
    ⅛ teaspoon salt
    1 cup margarine
    ⅓ cup firmly packed dark brown
      sugar
    ⅔ cup dark corn syrup

1. In large bowl, combine flour, cinnamon, nutmeg, cloves, and salt.
2. In large bowl, with mixer set at medium speed, beat margarine until soft. Gradually beat in sugar. Beat in corn syrup until well blended. Reduce speed to low and gradually beat in flour mixture until well mixed.
3. Cover and refrigerate several hours.

CUTTING AND BAKING

Hint: one batch of dough fills 2 cookie sheets. You will be preparing and baking a total of 6 sheets, but you can probably only bake 2 at a time. So, unless you have lots of bowls and cookie sheets, prepare, bake, and cool one batch at a time. You can of course roll out another batch of dough or even 2 to size on pieces of aluminum foil, then slide foil onto cardboard or large trays to refrigerate, and transfer them to the cookie sheets after the first batch is cooled and removed.

1. Line 12 x 15½-inch cookie sheets with foil.
2. Place 2⅓ cups dough on each sheet.
3. Roll out dough on each sheet to an 11 x 15-inch rectangle, ¼-inch thick.
4. Cover and refrigerate at least 30 minutes.
5. Cut out pieces and remove excess dough.
6. Fit tracing paper pattern over each cookie, and with a pin, prick pinholes through the paper into dough along all detail lines.
7. To make logs, roll excess dough into 2 ropes, each ⅜-inch thick by 10-inches long. Cut into 2-inch lengths. Place on foil-lined cookie sheet.
8. Place 2 cookie sheets at a time in oven and bake at 400°F 8 to 10 minutes or until edges are lightly browned. Cool completely before removing from foil.

DECORATING

1. Prepare 3 batches Royal Icing

following recipe in Basic Skills chapter.
2. Following pinholes made before baking, ice the pieces. Refer to color photograph, but don't be afraid to make whatever decorating changes suit your fancy.
3. Let all pieces dry completely before assembling, about 4 hours.

MAKING THE BASE

1. Cut a stiff, flat base 20 x 24 inches.
2. Cover base with foil.
3. Spread entire base with white Flow Frosting to resemble snow. Sprinkle shredded coconut over frosting before it dries for an even more wintry look.

ASSEMBLING THE BARN

1. On back and 1 side of barn, pipe white icing along side and bottom edges.
2. Carefully stand the back and side wall pieces on base, placing edge of side wall against inside edge of back wall. Spread extra icing on inside seams for additional strength. Fill in any seam irregularities with icing. Hold or prop in place with food cans until set, about 5 minutes.
3. Attach each of the other 2 walls in the same way. Let icing holding walls set at least 15 minutes before removing props.
4. Pipe white icing along top edge of front wall and adjoining top edges of side walls. On roof piece, spread icing along edges where roof and wall pieces will meet. Hold in place about 5 minutes or until set.
5. Pipe icing along seam edge where roof pieces meet. Then repeat procedure 4 for other roof piece. Let dry completely (about 4 hours).
6. Working with 1 piece at a time, pipe small amount of icing on long edge of window and shutter. Press each shutter in place next to window. Hold in place 5 minutes or until set.
7. Repeat procedure 6 for barn doors.

ATTACHING THE WOODSHED

1. Spread small amount of white icing along barnside edge of woodshed front and back pieces. Carefully position pieces 2½-inches apart against side of barn with no windows. Hold in place until set.

2. Spread icing along exposed edges of woodshed front and back. Place woodshed side against iced edges and hold until set.

3. Spread icing on top edges of front, side, and back pieces. Place roof on top and hold until set.

4. Fill woodshed with logs and store spare logs in refrigerator or airtight container to re-fill shed as passersby snitch logs.

ATTACHING THE FENCE

1. Spread icing along right edge of 10-inch long fence back. Carefully position at back corner of barn. Hold until set. Spread small amount of icing along left edge of fence side. Attach at left side of fence back. Hold until set. Spread icing along left edge of fence front. Attach to fence side piece and hold until set.

2. Spread icing along right edge of gate. Attach at front corner of barn so gate is open. Hold until set.

ATTACHING ANIMALS, FARMER, AND SLEIGH

1. Spread small amount of icing on bottom edges of animals, farmer, and sleigh, and place them upright on individual stands. Hold until set.

2. Arrange figures and sleigh as shown in photograph.

3. Add another reinforcing layer of icing around feet of figures and where sleigh's runners meet base.

4. Sprinkle artificial snow, shredded coconut, or confectioner's sugar over entire arrangement to complete the wintry scene.

These are full-sized patterns.

Small tree (cut 3)

Farmer

Large tree (cut 3)

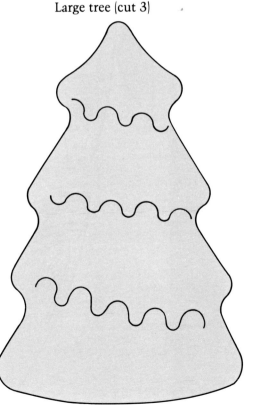

Wreath

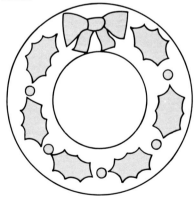

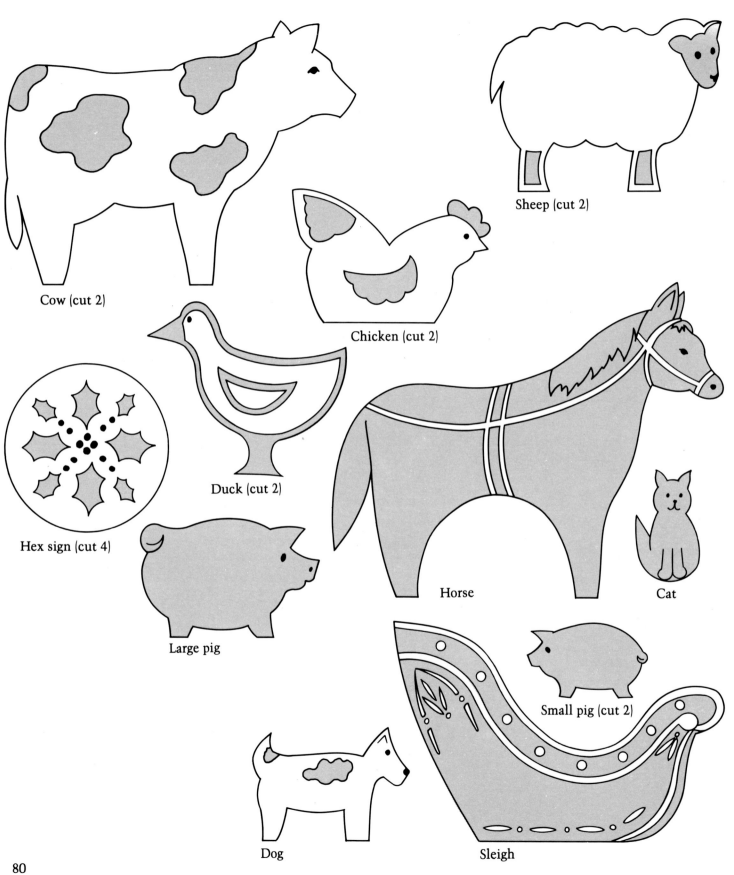

Cow (cut 2)

Sheep (cut 2)

Chicken (cut 2)

Hex sign (cut 4)

Duck (cut 2)

Large pig

Horse

Cat

Small pig (cut 2)

Dog

Sleigh

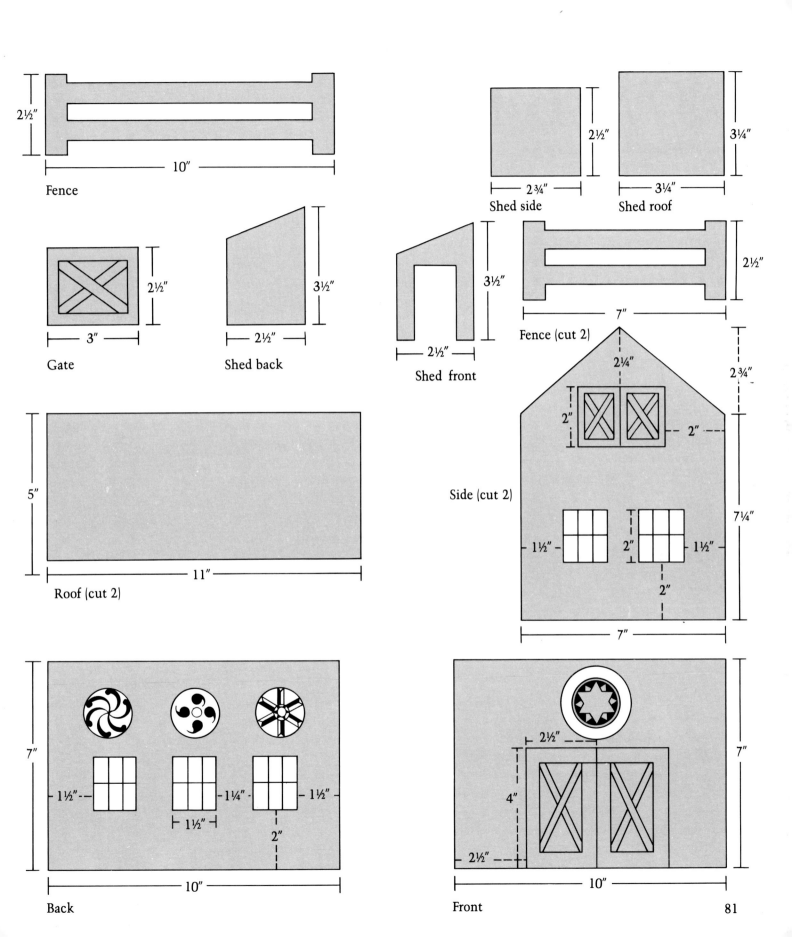

2½"
10"

Fence

2½"
3"

Gate

3½"
2½"

Shed back

5"
11"

Roof (cut 2)

7"
1½"
1½"
1¼"
1½"
2"
10"

Back

2½"
2¾"

Shed side

3¼"
3¼"

Shed roof

3½"
2½"

Shed front

2½"
7"

Fence (cut 2)

Side (cut 2)

2¼"
2"
2"
2"
1½"
1½"
2"
2¾"
7¼"
7"

2½"
4"
2½"
7"
10"

Front

81

Flower Tea

Gingerbread is such a versatile medium it can be woven into lattice and twisted into ropes for handles. The pentagonal centerpiece basket holds sixteen different flowers. A wire stem has been cemented to the undecorated back of each flower with Royal Icing so the flowers can be arranged into a bouquet with the help of a green styrofoam block inside the basket. Each place setting has a small, lattice basket with a lid, and a placecard edged with twisted ginger-braid. The name is written in Royal Icing. Fill each guest's basket with mints, tiny cookies, chocolates, or whatever comfit suits the occasion. Wouldn't it make a pretty garden party, a shower, or simply a celebration of a nice spring afternoon?

For flowers, make patterns and
mark design details. Use the full-sized
color illustrations as your guide.

For flowers, make patterns and
mark design details. Use the full-sized
color illustrations as your guide.

For flowers, make patterns and
mark design details. Use the full-sized
color illustrations as your guide.

YOU WILL NEED:
1 batch Basic Corn Syrup Gingerbread
   dough
1 batch Royal Icing; Flow Frosting

For flowers:
Food coloring in a variety of hues
Florist's wire for stems
Green styrofoam base

For small basket:
Comfit of your choice

MAKING THE PATTERNS
1. For flowers, make patterns and
mark design details following
instructions in Basic Skills chapter.
Use the full-sized color illustrations as
your guide.
2. The patterns for the large and small
baskets (except the handle) and the
placecards are shown in reduced
dimensions. To make full-sized
patterns, follow instructions in
Basic Skills chapter for enlarging
patterns.

Make tracing paper and cardboard
patterns for large basket bottom, small
basket bottom and lid, and for placecards, following instructions in Basic
Skills chapter. Make only waxed-paper
patterns for large basket sides (cut 5),
small basket sides (cut 5), and handle
(cut 2).

MIXING THE DOUGH
Prepare 1 batch Basic Corn Syrup
Gingerbread Dough, following recipe in
Basic Skills chapter. This will make
enough for 16 flowers, 1 large basket,
and 4 small baskets and placecards.

CUTTING, BAKING, AND
DECORATING THE FLOWERS
Roll out dough, cut out pieces and
mark design details, bake, and decorate

flowers following instructions in Basic
Skills chapter, using the color
illustrations as guides.

CUTTING AND BAKING
THE LARGE BASKET
1. Roll out dough on a large foil-
covered cookie sheet to a thickness of
¼ inch.
2. Cut out basket bottom following
instructions in Basic Skills chapter.
3. Cut twenty-five 5 x ½-inch and
twenty-five 4 x ½-inch strips of dough.
4. Place 5 large basket side waxed-
paper patterns on foil-lined cookie
sheet.
5. Evenly space five 5 x ½-inch strips of
dough 1 inch apart on each waxed-
paper pattern.
6. Weave five 4 x ½-inch strips over
and under each set of 5-inch strips,
taking care not to stretch or pull
dough.
7. Make ten 6 x ¼-inch rolls of dough,
then twist 2 of the rolls together and
place on top of each woven side.
8. Bake woven sides and basket
bottom in 350°F oven 10 to 15 minutes
or until lightly brown and set. Cool
completely before removing sides from
waxed paper.

ASSEMBLING
THE LARGE BASKET
1. Using pastry bag or parchment cone
and writing tip, pipe Royal Icing along
1 edge of basket bottom and position
bottom of 1 side piece in icing at a
right angle. Hold in place until set,
about 5 minutes.
2. Pipe icing along side of positioned
side piece and along next edge of
bottom and secure second woven side.
Hold until set. Repeat for 3 remaining
sides.
3. After icing seams have set, cover
them with a line of decorative icing
applied with a small star tip. Allow to

dry completely, about 4 hours.

MAKING THE HANDLE
1. Make four 12 x ½-inch rolls of
dough. Twist 2 rolls together, then the
other 2, and place on waxed-paper
patterns.
2. Bake the 2 twisted rolls in 350°F
oven 10 to 15 minutes. Cool
completely before removing from
waxed paper.
3. With decorator's tip, pipe icing on
flat side of 1 twisted roll and position
flat side of other twisted roll on it.
Allow to dry completely.
4. Ice florist's wire to flowers to make
stems, put styrofoam base in bottom of
basket, and, after icing has dried
completely, arrange flowers in basket.
5. Pipe icing on both ends of handle
and position on top of basket. Hold in
place until set, then allow to dry
completely.

MAKING THE SMALL BASKET
Make 1 for each guest.

1. Cut fifteen 3 x ½-inch and twenty
2 x ½-inch strips of dough for woven
sides.
2. Make ten 4 x ¼-inch rolls of dough
for top edges.
3. For knob on lid, roll some dough
into a small ball and position it in
center of lid.
4. Follow cutting, baking, and
assembly instructions for large basket.

MAKING PLACECARDS
Make 1 for each guest.

1. Make two 10 x ¼-inch rolls of
dough, twist together, and position on
top of placecard front. Bake as directed
above.
2. Attach support following
instructions in Basic Skills chapter.
3. Pipe guest's name on placecard in
icing using writing tip.

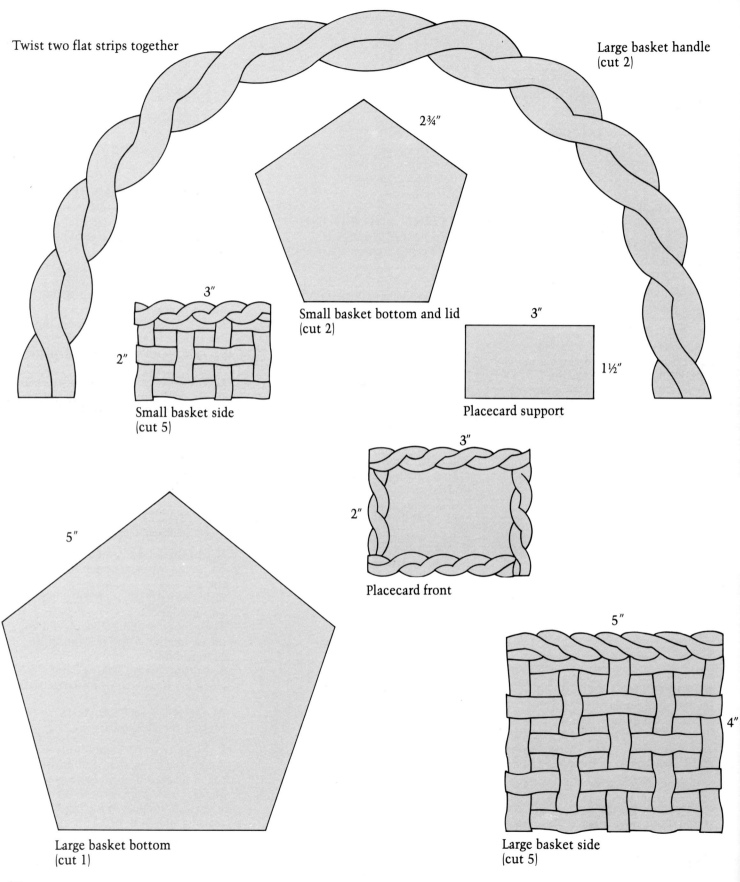

Twist two flat strips together

Large basket handle
(cut 2)

2¾"

Small basket bottom and lid
(cut 2)

3"

2"

Small basket side
(cut 5)

3"

1½"

Placecard support

3"

2"

Placecard front

5"

Large basket bottom
(cut 1)

5"

4"

Large basket side
(cut 5)

Noah's Ark

Still room on the ark? The supplies are on board; so are most of the animals. (The snakes have made nests for themselves in the shredded wheat on the roof.) The rest of the animals are pushing and shoving toward the ramp. But where are the turtles? Probably frightened by the lightning. It would be just like them to stop wherever they are, pull in their heads, and prepare to tough it out. Noah has gone off to look for them before it's too late. Better hurry, Noah! (He must have found them because we still have turtles today.)

YOU WILL NEED:

See Basic Skills chapter for general equipment and materials you will need for baking and decorating, and for propping structures to dry them.

1 batch Basic Corn Syrup Gingerbread Dough
1 batch Royal Icing; Flow Frosting

In addition, have on hand shredded wheat, waxed paper or clear plastic wrap, square blocks to prop braces at right angles while drying, full food cans for propping structures.

A base about 20 x 24 inches cut out of ¼-inch plywood or heavy cardboard if centerpiece is to be portable.

Mirror or clear plastic sheet to give the effect of water.

MAKING THE PATTERNS, CUTTING, AND BAKING

Make patterns for ark and animals, mix and roll out dough, cut out cookie pieces and mark design details, and bake following instructions in Basic Skills chapter. Be sure to mark dotted lines on undecorated insides of hull pieces and top of deck piece. These lines show where to attach other pieces to hull.

DECORATING

1. Prepare Royal Icing and mix Flow Frosting, following directions in Basic Skills chapter.
2. Following pattern markings and color illustration, decorate all pieces with icing and frosting except roof of house. See Basic Skills chapter.

ASSEMBLING THE HULL

1. Place one of the curved hull pieces, with portholes in it, on a towel or other soft, flat surface, decorated side down.
2. Pipe a line of icing along dotted line across bottom as shown in pattern.
3. Take one of the three 5-inch square bottom and end braces and position one edge in the line of icing. Prop it at right angles to hull piece with a square block wrapped with waxed paper on either side. Leave it undisturbed until icing sets (about 5 minutes).
4. In the same way, fix square pieces for two end braces in place on their dotted line, first one then the other. These act as braces to join the two sides together. The deck rests on the two end pieces so they must be even or the deck will slant.
5. Prop all three pieces and leave them to dry in a protected spot for about 4 hours. Remove props before proceeding with assembly. If you can't wait 4 hours, you must be very, very gentle with the next step.
6. Put deck piece where you can reach it quickly. Pipe icing along thin edges of the bow, stern, and bottom pieces that face up toward you. Lower other side of hull in position onto the frosted edges, with decorated side facing up toward you. Use the dotted positioning lines (especially the bottom line) as guides to position the two sides evenly without disturbing the hull. Quickly and gently slide the deck piece in place, to be sure it will fit later, then remove it again.
7. Leave the assembled pieces as they are in a protected spot to dry thoroughly. Meanwhile, assemble deck house.

ASSEMBLING THE DECK HOUSE

1. Assemble 4 walls of deck house following instructions in Basic Skills chapter.
2. Spread roof with white Flow Frosting and crumble shredded wheat on top, to resemble thatching, while frosting is still wet.
3. When walls have dried hard, place deck piece, decorated side up, on work surface. Pipe icing along bottom edges of all 4 walls. Lower house into position in center of deck (see dotted lines on pattern piece).
4. Pipe a line of Royal Icing along slanted sides of one side of roof and position one roof piece on top. Hold and prop in place. Repeat for other roof piece. Allow to dry thoroughly.
5. Meanwhile, position animals inside hull looking out portholes. Hold them in place with a spot of Royal Icing if necessary. Attach lions to gangway with Royal Icing. Attach snakes to top of roof. Attach supports to undecorated sides of remaining animals after Flow Frosting and Royal Icing decorations on front side have dried. One monkey will not need a support if it is hung by the tail from side of ark as shown in photograph.

FINISHING TOUCHES

1. Prepare final location for centerpiece setting, or a stiff portable board to serve as a base on which it can be carried. A mirror or sheet of clear plastic on the surface will suggest water.
2. When hull has dried, place it in position on base and lower deck assembly onto it.
3. Fit end of gangway into notch on side of ark as shown in photograph, then position animals and bags of feed. Use a dab of Royal Icing to hold pieces in position as necessary.

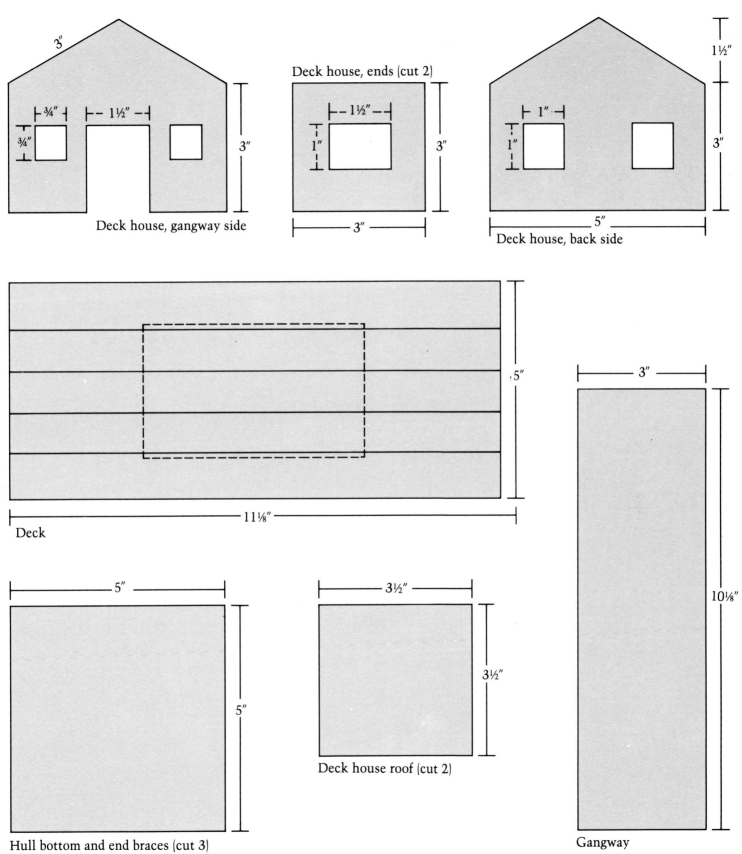

3"

Deck house, gangway side

¾"   1½"

¾"

3"

Deck house, ends (cut 2)

1½"

1"

3"

3"

Deck house, back side

1½"

1"

1"

3"

5"

Deck

5"

11⅛"

Hull bottom and end braces (cut 3)

5"

5"

Deck house roof (cut 2)

3½"

3½"

Gangway

3"

10⅛"

91

Pattern is shown folded back on itself to fit on this page, full sized.

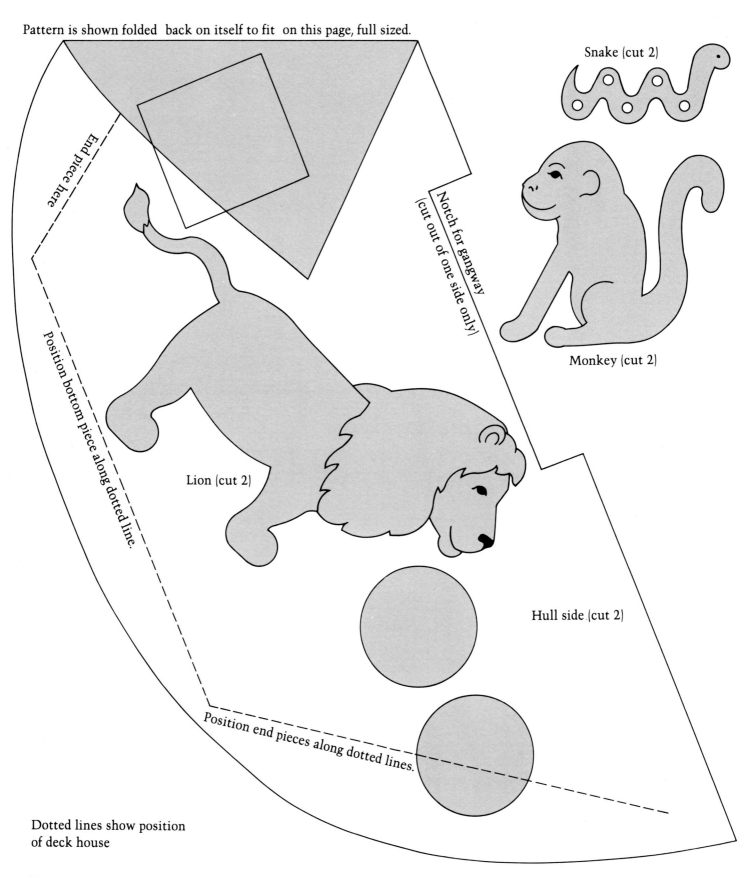

Snake (cut 2)

Monkey (cut 2)

End piece here

Position bottom piece along dotted line.

Notch for gangway
(cut out of one side only)

Lion (cut 2)

Hull side (cut 2)

Position end pieces along dotted lines.

Dotted lines show position
of deck house

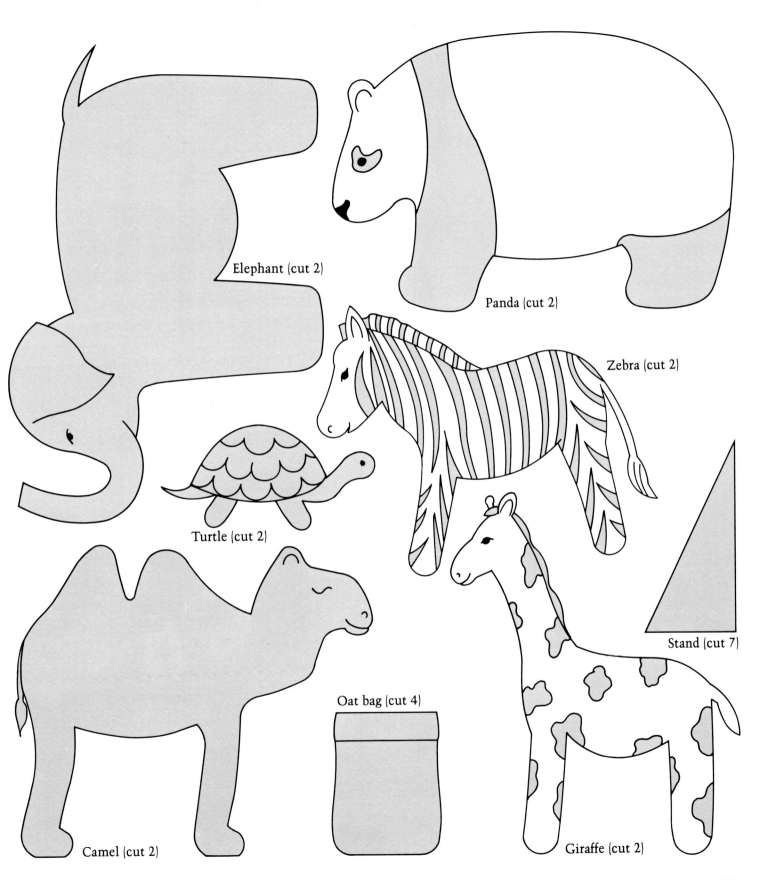

Elephant (cut 2)

Panda (cut 2)

Zebra (cut 2)

Turtle (cut 2)

Stand (cut 7)

Oat bag (cut 4)

Camel (cut 2)

Giraffe (cut 2)

93

the MONsters' picnic

Children are invited! The monsters
are having a picnic and they'd just love
to have a group of kids join them. Kids
understand monsters better than adults
do. (From the monster's viewpoint, being
scary is the whole game, and most
adults have forgotten how to go wide-
eyed and happily wriggly-scared.)
There'll be lots of fun and lots of food,
but warn the kids: If they behave like
monsters they may end up like that
small monster in the claws of the huge
orange one lounging lazily in the grass.
He was getting ready to chomp down on
a still smaller monster while about to be
swallowed by the biggest monster of
them all.

These are the full-sized patterns for the small cookies in The Monsters' Picnic.

The largest monster is decorated on both sides so you can use him as a centerpiece. The smaller monsters may be decorated according to the picture, or you may want to invent your own design. Two cookies of the same shape can be made to look very different, as you see. Since monsters can handle children, and vice versa, they make a successful theme for a young child's birthday party, especially if it is a picnic-party (where even the monsters can relax because spilling doesn't count.) Imagine bringing along these monster cookies as a surprise. Wrap them individually in paper or cloth towels and pack them in their own basket. Nobody is allowed to peek until you all get to the picnic place and set them up in the soft grass (where they won't chip if a wayward breeze or a curious four-year-old tips them over.) To keep the centerpiece intact bake up a batch of undecorated (but equally tasty) monster cookies for the human diners.

YOU WILL NEED:
1 batch Basic Honey Gingerbread Dough
1 batch Royal Icing; Flow Frosting

PREPARING THE PATTERNS
1. Following instructions in Basic Skills chapter, trace the full-sized patterns for large, reclining cookie monster onto tracing paper, cut out paper pattern, then make and cut out cardboard patterns.

Note: the right arm is a separate piece, holding a small, decorated monster cookie which, in turn, is about to eat an even smaller, undecorated monster.

2. Copy the design details onto the tracing paper pattern, using the color photograph as a guide. If you want to use the large monster as a counterpiece, make 2. Each will be decorated on one side and glued together with Royal Icing, so the centerpiece may be viewed from either side.

3. Make tracing paper and cardboard patterns for the 2 small monster cookies by tracing the full-sized color photographs, then mark design details on tracing paper patterns. Note that the same shapes may be decorated differently, as shown in the photographs.

MIXING, CUTTING, BAKING, AND DECORATING
Prepare Basic Honey Gingerbread Dough and Royal Icing following instructions in Basic Skills chapter. You will also find the directions in the Basic Skills chapter for cutting out cookie pieces and marking design details, and for baking and decorating the cookies.

Hint: bake up an extra batch of the small monster cookies so young human guests at the Monster's Picnic can gobble up those monsters instead of the decorated centerpiece.

Make 1 support for each small monster, in the shape of a right triangle, 2½ inches at the base and 3½ inches high.

Make 2 supports for large reclining monster by cutting two semicircles, each 4½ inches in diameter. Cut a notch 1 inch deep out of center of rounded edge of each semicircle. It should be wide enough to hold 2 thicknesses of decorated cookie.

ASSEMBLING THE MONSTERS
1. Decorate the small monsters and the 2 sides and 2 supports of the large monster with Flow Frosting and Royal Icing.
2. Spread a soft towel on work surface and lay 1 of the large monster pieces on it, decorated side down. Spread Royal Icing thickly on the undecorated side with a rubber or metal spatula, and fill in hollows.
3. Place the undecorated side of the other cookie on icing, matching contours, like an icing sandwich.

Hint: since large cookies warp in baking, fill in uneven spaces with Royal Icing.

4. Allow icing to dry completely

(about 4 hours) before attaching arm pieces with a dab of Royal Icing.

5. Attach arm piece on one side as shown in photograph, so reclining monster appears to be about to eat the monsters in its fist. Allow first arm piece to dry before attaching matching arm piece on other side.

6. Slip reclining monster into notches of 2 semicircular supports at elbow and ankle.

7. Attach triangular supports to undecorated sides of small monsters.

(cut 1 then reverse and cut 1)

(cut 1 then reverse and cut 1)

FINISHING TOUCHES
Put the centerpiece in place on your table or set it up at the picnic area. Arrange more plain or decorated cookies on serving plate and wait for the smiles to appear on those eager human faces.

CIRCUS TRAIN

Nobody has noticed, but the door at the end of the first car, which houses the lions and tigers, has swung open and one of the tigers has *escaped*! The animals know what's happened, but they're all searching for the missing tiger on the wrong side of the train. One of the chimps is climbing out of the caboose window so she can scamper over the roofs of the cars up to the engine and warn the engineer. He's preoccupied waving to the children who have gathered along the tracks at the edge of town to watch the circus train go by.

COMING SOON

The four-car circus train is finished on all sides, making it an ideal centerpiece. Picture it chugging down the middle of a birthday party table as guests return from an afternoon at the circus. Lift off the roofs of the cars to see the animals inside, but be careful because the icing and frosting chip off easily

To replicate the display in the photograph, trace and color the tiger pattern and glue it to a block of wood so it will stand up. Scatter hay in a thin layer (so the wheels will show) and pile some up behind and around the picture of the tiger.

YOU WILL NEED:

See Basic Skills chapter for general equipment and materials

2 batches Basic Corn Syrup
   Gingerbread Dough
1 batch Royal Icing; Flow Frosting

Blue, green, red, and yellow food coloring
2 mint candies; marshmallow

A stiff, flat base made of ¼-inch plywood or heavy cardboard, about 8½ x 14 inches. Or, you can use a spare tray.

MAKING THE PATTERNS

The patterns for the 4 cars of the Circus Train are shown in reduced dimensions. To make full-sized patterns, use ruler to enlarge shapes to sizes indicated. See Basic Skills chapter for instructions.

1. Make tracing paper patterns of all train car pieces shown on pattern page, following instructions in Basic Skills chapter. Be sure to indicate window and door openings.
2. In addition, see pattern page for dimensions of plain rectangles and circles to be used as roof, floor, wheel, and boiler pieces. Draw, cut out, and label each pattern as you finish it.
3. Trace patterns of animals and clown on tracing paper. These are full-sized and do not need enlarging.
4. Duplicate all patterns on cardboard following instructions in Basic Skills chapter.

MIXING THE DOUGH

Prepare 2 batches of Basic Corn Syrup Gingerbread Dough, following recipe in Basic Skills chapter.

CUTTING AND BAKING

Cut out pieces, mark clown and animal design details, and bake following instructions in Basic Skills chapter.

DECORATING

1. Prepare and tint Royal Icing following recipe in Basic Skills chapter. You will have 5 bowls of icing, white and the 4 colors.
2. Mix Flow Frosting from Royal Icing, following instructions in Basic Skills chapter.
3. Decorate animal pieces and clown with Royal Icing and Flow Frosting, using as guides the lines you pricked into dough before baking.
4. Use color photograph as guide for decorating and coloring train parts. See Basic Skills chapter for instructions on applying icing and frosting.

ASSEMBLING THE ELEPHANTS

1. Pipe icing along front edge of elephant body piece, position against middle of rear side of head piece, and hold until icing sets, about 5 minutes.
2. Pipe icing along both sides of seam as reinforcement and allow to dry completely, about 4 hours.

ASSEMBLING THE ENGINE

1. Using pastry bag or parchment cone and medium plain round decorator's tip, pipe icing along front vertical edge of engine side B and press against inside of left vertical edge of engine front A. Hold in place until set.
2. In same way, join opposite side B to front A and hold in place until set.

Note: place head and arm of decorated clown engineer through window opening before going on to next step.

3. Pipe icing along exposed vertical edges of sides B, put engine back C into position, and hold in place until set.
4. Pipe icing along top edges of all 4

pieces A, B, and C. Place roof E on top and hold in place until set.

5. To complete box shape, pipe icing along inside edges of engine bottom D, place engine cab on D, and hold in place until set.

6. To complete engine, use spatula or knife to spread icing on 1 of 12 boiler pieces F and place another piece F on top. Continue in this way until 12-cookie boiler is complete. Allow stack to dry completely.

7. Turn stack on side and spread icing on bottom of last cookie. Place against engine front A so stack rests on engine bottom D. Allow to dry completely.

8. Pipe icing on undecorated side of large wheel J and place at lower back edge of engine side B. Let icing set. In same way, attach 3 other large wheels, allowing 2 forward wheels to extend beyond front edge of side B.

9. Attach 2 small wheels K to either side of engine bottom D with icing. The distance between the centers of rear large wheel and small wheel should be about 4″. Let dry completely.

10. Ice inside of both ends of shaft L and attach to center of rear large wheel

and center of small wheel. In same way, attach second shaft L on other side. Allow to dry completely.

11. Pipe icing on undecorated side of cowcatcher side H, attach to lower front of engine front F. Hold in place until set. In same way, attach second cowcatcher side H to opposite side.

12. To strengthen cowcatcher assembly, pipe icing along 2 short sides of cowcatcher front I and position against inside lower edges of cowcatcher sides H.

13. Finish assembly by applying icing to 2 mint candies and attaching them to engine fronts as headlights. Ice 1 flat side of marshmallow and attach to top of engine front as smokestack.

ASSEMBLING THE CAGE CAR

1. Pipe icing along 1 long edge of cage bottom Q, press against bottom edge of cage side N, and hold in place until set.

2. Repeat to attach opposite side.

3. Pipe icing along front edges of cage sides and bottom, press cage front M against them, and hold in place until set.

4. Repeat to attach cage back.

5. Before attaching roof, put tiger and the lion's body without its head inside with neck sticking out between bars. Then use icing to attach lion's head. Hold in place until set.

6. Pipe icing along long edge of roof O. Position decoration piece P against it at right angle and hold in place until set. Repeat for other side of roof and let set. Put roof in place without icing. Removable roof permits viewing and rearranging animals.

7. Use icing to attach wheels, allowing half of wheel to extend below edge of wagon.

8. For reinforcement and decoration, pipe icing along 4 vertical seams of wagon.

ASSEMBLING THE ELEPHANT CAR

Follow previous sets of steps for assembling basic box shape and attaching wheels. There is no roof on this car. Reinforce and decorate seams. Place decorated, assembled elephants in finished car.

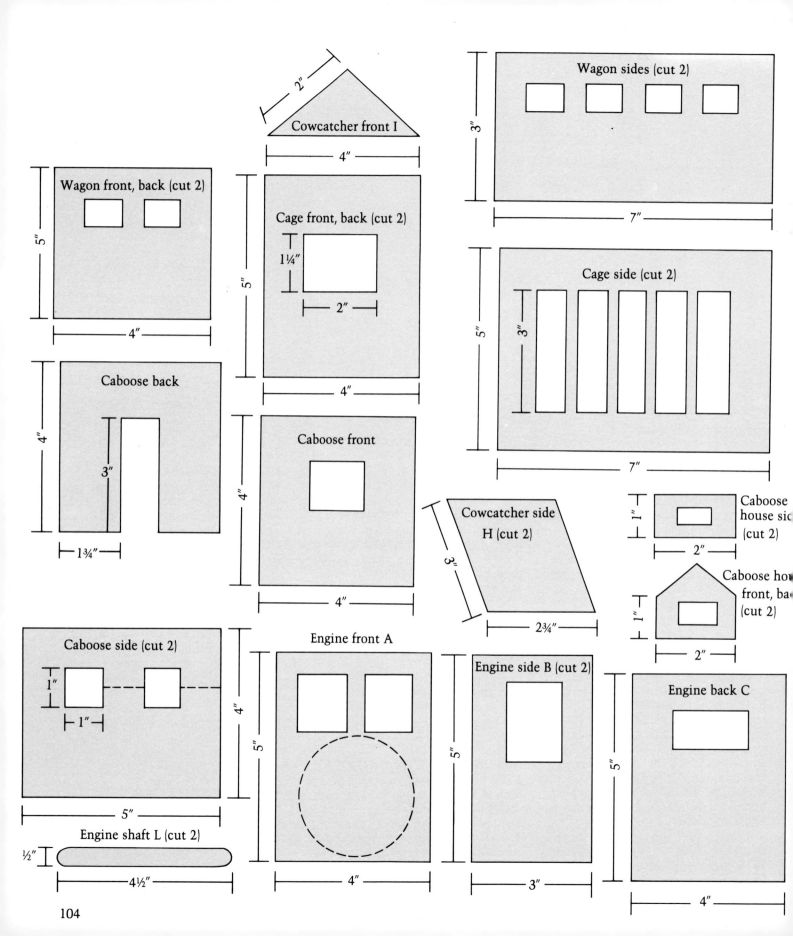

Cowcatcher front I

2″

4″

Wagon front, back (cut 2)

5″

4″

Wagon sides (cut 2)

3″

7″

Cage front, back (cut 2)

1¼″

2″

5″

4″

Cage side (cut 2)

5″

3″

7″

Caboose back

4″

3″

1¾″

Caboose front

4″

4″

Cowcatcher side
H (cut 2)

3″

2¾″

Caboose
house side
(cut 2)

1″

2″

Caboose house
front, back
(cut 2)

1″

2″

Caboose side (cut 2)

1″

1″

5″

Engine front A

4″

5″

4″

Engine side B (cut 2)

5″

3″

Engine back C

5″

4″

Engine shaft L (cut 2)

½″

4½″

Cage decoration piece P   (cut 2)

Caboose decoration piece (cut 2)

ASSEMBLING THE CABOOSE

Follow above steps for assembling caboose, attaching roof decorations and wheels, and for assembling roof house. Use icing to attach roof house to caboose roof and monkey to caboose side. Reinforce and decorate seams.

FINISHING TOUCHES

Trace and color full-page tiger's head picture and use straw or grass, real or artificial, to create background.

Caboose wheels in photo have "tinted glass" hubs requiring special treatment and baking. (See Making the "Tinted Glass" Candy and Cutting and Baking, Steps 7 to 9, in Village Church project.) For simpler treatment, pipe decorative icing as shown, but leave wheels solid.

Not shown. Make cardboard patterns of each of the following rectangles and circles:
Engine bottom D, 4" x 8"
Engine roof E, 5" x 5"
Boiler piece F, 3" circle (cut 12)
Large wheel J, 2½" circle (cut 4)
Small wheel K, 1¾" circle (cut 14)
Cage roof O, 8" x 4½"
Cage bottom Q, 7" x 3¾"
Wagon bottom, 7" x 3¾"
Caboose roof, 5" x 6"
Caboose bottom, 5" x 3¾"
Caboose house roof, 3" x 1½" (cut 2)

FAIRY TALES & TOYS

CONTENTS

the House of CATS

They say that old London
has plenty of flats

Of both hot- and cold-water
variety, that's

Peopled not only by
persons but cats.

They claw up the draperies,
nestle in hats

Arch over chimney pots
howl back at brats,

Dominate ottomans
rub against spats,

And purr unexpectedly
loudly at bats.

YOU WILL NEED

See Basic Skills chapter for general equipment and materials.

In addition, have on hand: dull knife or spatula; toothpicks; cellophane or masking tape; ¼-inch artist's paintbrush; plastic wrap; brown paper; full food cans; small empty boxes; felt tip marker.

2 batches Dark Gingerbread Dough
1 batch Light Gingerbread Dough
1 batch Royal Icing; Flow Frosting
1 batch Molasses Frosting

Blue, pink, yellow, green food coloring

MAKING THE PATTERNS

Most patterns for House of Cats are shown full-sized, but patterns for house front and side are illustrated in reduced dimensions. Follow instructions in Basic Skills chapter for tracing and enlarging patterns, and for making cardboard patterns.

Note: be sure to make 2 house side patterns, one with both windows (right side), and one with top window only (left side). Mark and cut out window openings.

MIXING THE DOUGH

Prepare 2 batches of Dark Gingerbread Dough and 1 batch of Light Gingerbread Dough, following recipes in Games chapter.

CUTTING THE PIECES

Pieces are cut of cardboard, dark dough, or light dough, or a combination of these 3. Refer to chart to find out how many pieces to cut of which material(s). Rather than working with all 3 materials at once, we suggest you first cut out and label cardboard pieces, then use these as patterns when cutting out dough pieces.

When you start to work with the dough, roll and cut only ½ batch (1 cookie sheet) at a time to avoid drying. Roll out dough on foil-lined cookie sheet following instructions in Basic Skills chapter, but roll to a thickness of ¹⁄₁₆ inch, rather than ¼ inch.

1. For pieces which have patterns,

follow instructions for cutting and marking design details in Basic Skills
2. For pieces which do not have patterns, first refer to chart for dimensions. Then, using ruler, a straight-edge, pencil (for cardboard only), and sharp knife or scissors, mark and cut pieces directly on dough or cardboard. Score or cut pieces as directed by notes on chart.

Code	Description	Dimensions (in inches)	Cardboard	Light Dough	Dark Dough
A	House front	See pattern	1	1[1]	1*
B	Right side	See pattern	1	1	1*
C	Left side	See pattern	1	1[2]	1*
D	Valence	2 x 2½			1
E	Door	2 x 3½			2*
F	Lintel/Basket	1½-inch circle			2
G	Closet pieces	1¼ x 4			4[3]
H	Coat	See pattern		1	
I	Pocket	See pattern		1	
J	Mother cat	See pattern		1	
K	First floor	12 x 6	1		1[4]
L	Roof pieces	8 x 7			2*
M	Stair treads	1½ x 10	1		
N	Stair sides	See pattern	2		1
O	Stair treads	1½ x 2	1		
P	Stair sides	See pattern	2		1
Q	Stair railing	See pattern	1		
R	Second floor[5]	12 x 6	1		1*
S	Attic floor	8¾ x 6	1		1*
T	Chimney front and back	See pattern	2		2
U	Chimney left side	1¼ x 1¾	1		1
V	Chimney right side	1¼ x 1⅛	1		1
W	First floor divider top	4 x ½	1		1
X	First floor divider	3½ x 2½	1	2	
Y	Second floor divider	3½ x 5¼	1	2	
Z	Bed center	2¼ x 2¾	2		
AA	Bed head	See pattern		1	1
BB	Bed foot	See pattern		1	1
CC	Chair center	¾ x 1	2		
DD	Chair back	See pattern		2	
EE	Chair front	See pattern		2	
FF	Chest front	1½ x 1¾			1*
GG	Chest sides	¾ x 1¾			2
HH	Chest top	1½ x ¾			1
II	Table leg	2 x 1½	1		
JJ	Table top	2½-inch circle		1	
KK	Table leg	1½ x ¾	1		
LL	Sofa center	See pattern	1		
MM	Sofa side	See pattern			2
NN	Sofa back	See pattern			1
OO	Closet top	1½ x 1			1*

*Score as shown in photograph.
[1] Cut 3 inches from top, and score a line 5½ inches from bottom.
[2] Cut off bottom 5½ inches.
[3] Score one piece only for door.
[4] Remove a 2½-inch circle from the center of the right side, and replace with a 2½-inch circle of light dough. Score dark dough to resemble flooring as shown in photograph.

[5] Remove a rectangle 2 inches wide by 3 inches high from one corner of both the cardboard and dark dough second floor pieces. This will be the stair opening.

MAKING AND ATTACHING THE SHUTTERS, CURTAINS, DOORS, AND MISCELLANY

Shutters and curtains are made from the window cutouts from pieces A, B, and C. (Remove cutouts carefully with a spatula, and chill for a few minutes if dough is too soft.) Doors and valances are cut out separately. All pieces are attached to pieces A, B, and C before baking by moistening their backs with a finger dipped in water then pressing them gently into position. They are then scored with a dull knife or spatula to simulate carving or draping.

1. Divide rectangular window cutouts from dark dough piece A in half lengthwise. Attach on either side of each window opening to make shutters and score carving.

Note: remove circular window cutout and reserve.

2. For upper left window of light dough piece A and upper window of light dough piece B, divide cutouts in quarters. Attach as above, overlapping each quarter to make tiered curtains. Score for drapery.

3. For upper right window of light dough piece A and upper window of piece C, divide cutouts in half lengthwise, and flare bottom of each half with fingers. Attach on either side of window openings to make curtains, and score for drapery.

4. For lower right window of light dough piece A and lower window of light dough piece C, divide cutouts in half lengthwise, attach on either side of window openings to make curtains, and score for drapery.

5. Use cutout from lower left window of light dough piece A for valances above windows in step 4 above. Score for drapery.

6. Attach piece D above lower left window of light dough piece A to make a valance.

7. Using pattern markings as a guide, attach one piece E and ½ of piece F to dark dough piece A to make exterior door and lintel, and second piece E to light dough piece A to make interior door. Score for carving and use dough scraps for door knobs.

8. Make cats of dough scraps and position climbing into windows, sitting on window sills, climbing the curtains or valances, or as you wish. Attach as above.

9. Attach pieces H and I to one piece G to make coat hanging on closet back. Mold a kitten head of dark dough scraps and attach to H/I unit so it looks like kitten is peering out of coat pocket.

10. Using dough scraps, mold 3 tiny kittens for basket of kittens in attic. Mold a kitten and place in mother cat's mouth (piece J), then mold a cat for the roof ridge. Mold "junk" for attic.

Note: to secure heads of upright cats, first insert piece of toothpick into body, then push head onto end of pick.

BAKING THE PIECES

1. Bake in 350°F oven 6 to 8 minutes or until cookie pieces are firm and lightly browned. Cool 5 minutes on cookie sheet.

2. You can check sizes of pieces by laying patterns on them while pieces are still warm. Trim areas that have expanded more than ⅛ inch beyond edges of patterns.

ASSEMBLING THE CARDBOARD HOUSE FRAME

1. Lay piece A on flat surface. Place B on right and C on left. Tape to A.

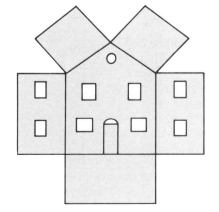

2. Tape K securely to bottom edge of A
3. Tape 8-inch edges of pieces L securely to peaked edges of A.
4. Lift up B, C, and K and tape at corners.
5. Lift up pieces L and tape together at peak, and to top edges of B and C.
6. Stand frame upright and tape around windows to make smooth edges.

ASSEMBLING THE CARDBOARD STAIRS

1. Starting 1 inch from one end and stopping 1½ inches from the other, draw lines across width of M at ½-inch intervals. Fold like a fan.
2. Beginning with 1-inch section, tape M to pieces N to make stair treads and risers.
3. Starting 1 inch from one end, draw 3 lines across width of O at ½-inch intervals.   Fold like a fan.

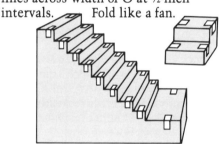

4. Beginning with 1-inch section, tape O to pieces P to make treads and risers.
5. Tape M/N unit to O/P unit at right angles.
6. Tape Q to what will be the outer edge of stairs, curving outward as you get to the bottom.

ASSEMBLING THE HOUSE

1. Prepare 1 batch Royal Icing following instructions in Basic Skills chapter. But before icing becomes stiff, reserve half of it in a covered bowl to use for Flow Frosting later. Beat remaining icing until stiff. Cover tightly, and set aside.
2. Pipe a line of frosting all around interior walls of cardboard house frame, 11 inches from the bottom. Paint area above line and attic ceiling by spreading frosting over it. Also paint lower left side of interior up to 5½ inches from the bottom, and bottoms of second floor and attic floor pieces. Let dry at least 45 minutes.

See Basic Skills chapter for instructions for applying Royal Icing.

3. Lay frame on its front so you're looking into interior of house from back. Spread thin layer of icing over interior of house front and press light cookie piece A into place. Repeat procedure with light pieces B, C, and K. Let dry at least 45 minutes.
4. Spread icing on right side of stair unit and press light pieces N and P into place.
5. Set house right side up. Cut seven 3-inch squares of plastic wrap, place over window holes on outside of house, and tape edges securely. Cut 14 very thin strips of brown paper, then place 2 over each window to divide it into panes. Tape securely.
6. Spread icing over outside of house and press dark pieces A, B, C, and L into place. Prop with full food cans and empty food boxes and let dry at least 45 minutes. See Basic Skills chapter for instructions on propping structures.
7. Measure cardboard pieces R and S to fit tightly into place. Very carefully trim dark pieces R and S to fit cardboard exactly and ice onto unfrosted sides of cardboard. Let dry at least 45 minutes.
8. Tape together cardboard pieces U and V to form chimney, then ice dark pieces U and V onto chimney.
9. Ice the two plain pieces G to inside sides of stairs. Trim piece G (with coat) to fit between sides and push into place. Turn stairs upside down and ice pieces G together.
10. Ice side and back edges of cardboard/gingerbread piece R. Fit into place so it is at level scored on light gingerbread piece A, and will meet top of stairs. Pipe a line of icing underneath floor to secure in place. Prop to hold in place.
11. Ice side and back edges of cardboard/gingerbread piece S and fit into place. Prop with small empty boxes placed on R directly above props placed under R. Secure with a line of icing underneath.
12. Assemble dividers: tape cardboard piece W on top of and perpendicular to cardboard piece X. Spread icing on both

sides of cardboard pieces W, X, and Y, and attach corresponding gingerbread pieces.

13. Ice cardboard/gingerbread chimney into place. Let house, dividers, and stairs dry overnight.

14. Remove props the next day. Spread icing on bottom edge of cardboard/gingerbread piece W/X, and on top and bottom edges and 1 side edge of cardboard/gingerbread piece Y. Ice into place as shown in color photograph.

ASSEMBLING AND PAINTING THE FURNITURE

1. Divide reserved Flow Frosting into 5 small bowls. Leave the contents of one white, and tint the others blue, pink, yellow, and green. See instructions in Basic Skills chapter for tinting and applying Flow Frosting.

2. For beds, fold in ½ inch on each 2¾-inch side of pieces Z for bed centers. Using ¼-inch paintbrush, paint one pink and the other blue. Frost centers between AA and BB with corresponding color.

3. For chairs, fold in ¼ inch on each 1-inch side of pieces CC for chair centers. Paint with yellow frosting and frost centers between DD and EE with yellow.

4. For chest, pipe white icing along back side edges of FF and push pieces GG into place. Hold until set, about 5 minutes. Ice bottom outside edges of HH and position on top of unit FF/GG. Hold until set.

5. For dining table, roll II around a thick felt tip marker and tape to make a 1½-inch center leg. Dot yellow frosting on one end and attach to JJ. Paint leg and center of table top with yellow frosting.

6. For coffee table, roll KK around a pencil and tape to make a ¾-inch high leg. Dot blue icing on one end and attach to reserved circular window cutout. Paint leg with blue frosting.

7. For sofa, fold LL along dotted lines to make sofa center. Attach to side pieces MM and back NN with blue frosting, then paint center blue.

DECORATING THE HOUSE

1. Paint stair treads with blue frosting, and stair railing with white frosting. Spread cardboard side of stairs with white icing and press into place against left side. Trim stair railing level with second floor.

2. Decorate curtains in upper left bedroom with pink as shown in photograph, and curtains in upper right bedroom with green.

3. Put white frosting in pastry bag with #1 or #2 decorator's tip. See instructions in Basic Skills chapter for using bag and tip. Pipe a lace border on yellow mat in center of table and decorations on shutters and above door as shown. Pipe eyes on cats, and knobs on door and chest. Pipe some white frosting under upstairs front windows and spread to make window boxes.

4. Paint rug cutout under dining table with yellow frosting.

5. Mix a little pink and yellow to make orange frosting. Paint some or all of the cats orange. With #1 or #2 decorator's tip, pipe white frosting eyes on cats and give them pink noses.

6. With white frosting, make a pillow on reserved piece F. Press molded kittens into frosting, and frost in place in attic. Make another pillow on second floor and press another cat into place.

7. Mix a little icing with the green frosting to stiffen it. Add more color if necessary. Using a leaf tip, pipe flower leaves along front, in window baskets, and on windowless bottom left side of house. Stiffen the other frosting colors with a little icing, and paint flowers among the leaves.

8. Using stiffened colored frosting and a medium star tip, pipe matching or contrasting pillows on bed.

FINISHING TOUCHES

1. Prepare 1 batch of Molasses Frosting.

In large bowl, combine 1¼ cups confectioners sugar, 1 egg white, and 1 tablespoon light or dark molasses and beat with electric mixer at high speed until stiff, fluffy, and caramel-colored.

2. Put Molasses Frosting in pastry bag

with adapter and a small star tip.

3. Pipe several rows of shell border at roof ridge, chimney edges, under eaves, at edges of all floors and dividers, around closet, under stairs, and anywhere else rough interior edges need to be covered.

Note: shell border is made by placing tip ¼-inch back from starting point and piping frosting forward to starting point, then back about ½ inch, repeating until border is completed.

4. Press closet door (last remaining piece G) into place and prop with pencil.

5. Press piece OO into place at top of closet as shown.

6. Position large cat in frosting on roof ridge.

7. Change to a medium star tip and pipe a border around top of stairs; then frost "junk" and mother cat (piece J) in place in attic.

8. Put furniture in place.

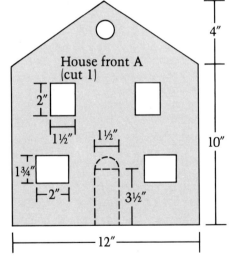

House front A (cut 1)

2" 1½" 1½" 1¾" 2" 3½" 12" 4" 10"

House side B and C (cut 1 with both windows (B) and one with top window only (cut 1) (C))

1½" 10" 6"

Sofa back NN
(cut 1)

Coat H
(cut 1)

Pocket

I

Stair railing Q (cut 1)

Stair side N
(cut 2)

Chimney T
(cut 1, turn
over and
cut another)

Stair side P
(cut 2)

Sofa center LL
(cut 1)

Bed head AA

Chair back DD
(cut 2)

Bed foot BB
(cut 2)

Chair front EE
(cut 2)

Sofa side MM
(cut 1, turn
over and cut
another)

Mother cat J
(cut 1)

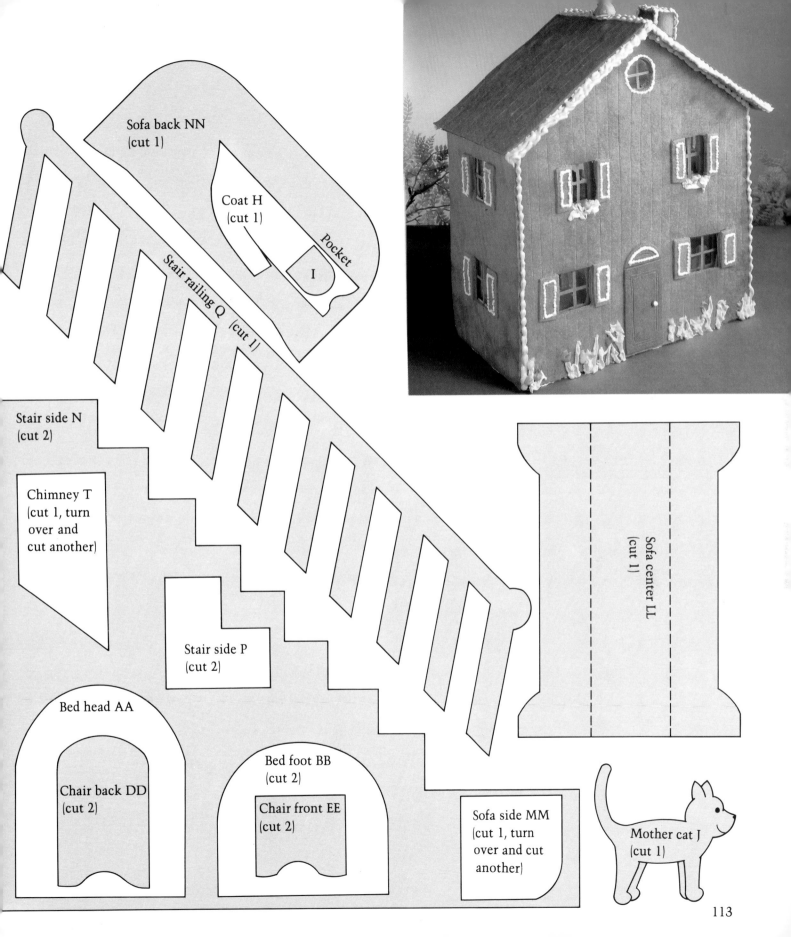

Witch's Cottage

YOU WILL NEED:

See Basic Skills chapter for general equipment and materials.

Edibles: Black licorice laces and strawberry licorice whips, fruit slices for rooftop, shutters, and door, gelatin for window curtains, Dutch chocolate mint lentils for path, peppermints, gumdrops, and pectin fruits for roof

3 egg whites and approximately 2 cups powdered sugar for glaze icing.
1 batch gingerbread dough
1 batch Royal Icing; Flow Frosting

Wood or heavy cardboard base large enough to hold cottage and figures (optional)

MAKING THE PATTERNS

Enlarge patterns for witch's cottage, transfer them onto light cardboard, and cut them out following instructions in Basic Skills chapter. You will use the cardboard patterns to cut out the cookie pieces and as permanent backing for the cottage walls and roof. The patterns for Hansel and Gretel and the Witch are full-size color photographs. Use the full size tree pattern. See the Basic Skills chapter for instructions on tracing and cutting out patterns. Also see that chapter for instructions on how to make patterns for supports for the figures so they will stand upright.

MIXING THE DOUGH

1 cup margarine
2 cups honey
1 cup sugar
1 teaspoon each cinnamon, ginger, and nutmeg
2 tablespoons cocoa
7½ cups flour
2 teaspoons baking soda
1 pinch salt
2 eggs

1. In saucepan, melt margarine. Add honey, sugar, spices, and cocoa, stirring constantly until sugar is dissolved. Let cool.
2. In large bowl, combine flour, baking soda, and salt.
3. Add eggs and cooled honey mixture and knead into smoothly textured dough. Place uncovered in refrigerator for about 2 hours.

CUTTING AND BAKING

1. Lightly flour rolling pin and roll out dough to ¼-inch thickness on well-greased cookie sheet.
2. Lay lightly floured cardboard patterns on dough and, using sharp pointed knife, cut around the outlines. Then cut out door and window openings, but save pieces to reattach to openings later.
3. Re-roll and cut out excess dough to make figures and trees.
4. Bake pieces at 350°F 10 to 12 minutes. Poke dough occasionally with fork to allow air to escape.
5. Remove cookies to a rack and cool.

DECORATING

1. For glaze icing, in a bowl mix 3 egg whites with enough powdered sugar (about 2 cups) so it can be applied with a parchment cone or pastry bag and tip in Basic Skills chapter. To prevent drying, keep bowl of icing covered with a damp cloth.
2. Using the color photograph as a guide for decorating the front of the cottage, pipe icing around openings for windows and door. Pipe icing on candy fruit slice shutters and position them on front wall. Put dot of icing above window and attach a peppermint candy. Decorate door piece with icing and candy fruit slice. Use your own imagination to decorate the back of the house.
3. Apply icing thickly to roof pieces and decorate with various candies. You can duplicate our candy arrangement or decorate to your own liking.
4. Prepare Royal Icing and mix and color instructions in Basic Skills chapter.
5. Decorate Hansel and Gretel, the Witch, and the trees with Royal Icing and Flow Frosting. See the Basic Skills chapter for instructions on applying icing and frosting. You can use the color photograph as your decorating guide, or suit your own fancy.

ASSEMBLING THE COTTAGE

1. Pipe icing onto cardboard patterns for walls and roof and attach to backs of baked pieces. Let dry completely (about 4 hours) before assembling cottage.
2. Cut a stiff base of wood or heavy cardboard large enough to hold the cottage and figures, or use a spare metal tray. If you are making a gingerbread base for the cottage alone, cut and bake one 10 inches square.
3. Pipe icing on bottom edges of 1 side wall, position on base, and hold in place until set, about 5 minutes.
4. Apply icing to edge of side wall adjoining back and to bottom edge of back wall and position back wall. Hold in place until set.
5. Position other side and front in the same way. If you need to prop the pieces, see instructions in Basic Skills chapter. Allow structure to dry completely.
6. Pipe icing along slanted edges of front and back walls and put roof piece into position. Prop if necessary. Let dry completely, then repeat for other roof piece.
7. Attach door and back window pieces with icing.
8. Reinforce outside corners and roof edges of cottage with decoratively piped icing, then, before icing dries, attach strawberry licorice whips with icing. Use the photograph as a guide.
9. Attach supports to the backs of standing figures with icing, following instructions in Basic Skills chapter.
10. Assemble trees using icing to attach the 2 slotted parts.
11. Arrange Hansel and Gretel, the Witch, the trees, and the gumdrop flowers and shrubs to complete the scene.

Roof (cut 2)

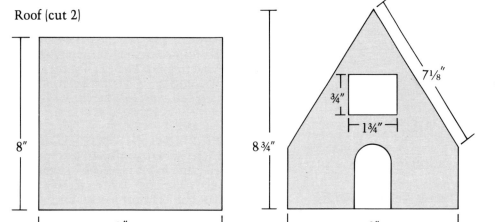

8"

9"

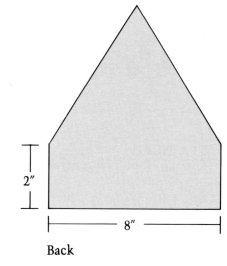

8 3/4"

3/4"

1 3/4"

7 1/8"

Front

2"

8"

Back

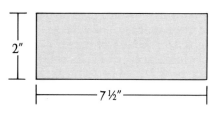

2"

7 1/2"

Side (cut 2)

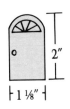

2"

1 1/8"

Tree

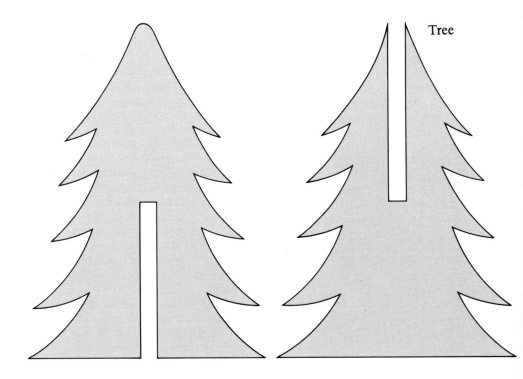

116

HANSEL AND GRETEL

ONCE upon a time there dwelt near a large wood a poor wood cutter with his wife and two children by his former marriage, a little boy called Hansel, and a girl named Gretel. He had little enough to break or bite, and once, when there was a great famine in the land, he could not procure even his daily bread; and as he lay thinking in his bed one evening, rolling about for trouble, he sighed, and said to his wife, "What will become of us? How can we feed our children when we have no more than we can eat ourselves?"

"Know, then, my husband," answered she, "we will lead them away quite early in the morning into the thickest part of the wood, and there make them a fire, and give them each a little piece of bread; then we will go to our work and leave them alone, so they will not find the way home again, and we shall be freed from them." The two children, however, had not gone to sleep for very hunger, and so they overheard what the stepmother said to their father.

Early in the morning the stepmother came and pulled them out of bed, and gave them each a slice of bread. On the way Hansel broke his in his pocket, and stopping every now and then, dropped a crumb upon the path.

The mother led the children deep into the wood, where they had never been before, and there making an immense fire she said to them, "Sit down here and rest, and when you feel tired you can sleep for a little while. We are going into the forest to hew wood, and in the evening, when we are ready, we will come and fetch you."

When noon came Gretel shared her bread with Hansel who had strewn his on the path. Then they went to sleep and in the dark night they awoke. The moon shone and they got up, but they could not see any crumbs, for the thousands of birds which had been flying about in the woods and fields had picked them all up.

They walked the whole night long and the next day, but still they did not come out of the wood; and they got so hungry, for they had nothing to eat but the berries which they found upon the bushes. They still walked on and on, but they only got deeper and deeper into the wood.

Suddenly they came into a cleared place in the forest and saw a cottage with a steep roof that reached almost to the ground. When they went close up to it they saw that the cottage was made of bread and cakes, and the window panes were of clear sugar. Hansel reached up and broke a piece off the roof, in order to see how it tasted; while Gretel stepped up to the window and began to bite it. Just then the door opened, and a very old woman, walking upon crutches, came out. Hansel and Gretel were so frightened that they let fall what they had in their hands; but the old woman, nodding her head, said, "Ah, you dear children, what has brought you here? Come in and stop with me, and no harm shall befall you."

The old woman behaved very kindly to them, but in reality she was a wicked witch who waylaid children, and built the bread-house in order to entice them in; but as soon as they were in her power she killed them, cooked and ate them, and made a great festival of the day. Witches have red eyes, and cannot see very far; but they have a fine sense of smelling, like wild beasts, so that they know when children approach them.

Early in the morning, before they awoke, the witch took up Hansel with her rough hand, and shut him up in a little cage with a lattice-door; and although he screamed loudly it was of no use. Gretel came next. "Get up you lazy thing, and fetch some water to cook something good for your brother, who must remain in that stall and get fat; when he is fat enough I shall eat him."

Every morning the old witch came to the cage and said, "Hansel, stretch out your finger that I may feel whether you are getting fat." But Hansel used to stretch out a bone, and the old woman, having very bad sight, thought it was his finger, and wondered very much that it did not get fat. When four weeks had passed, and Hansel still kept quite lean, she lost all her patience and would not wait any longer. "Gretel," she called out in a passion, "get some water quickly; be Hansel fat or lean, this morning I will kill and cook him."

So early in the morning Gretel was forced to go out and fill the kettle, and make a fire. "First we will bake, however," said the old woman; "I have already heated the oven and kneaded the dough;" and so saying she pushed poor Gretel up to the oven, out of which the flames were burning fiercely. "Creep in," said the witch, "and see if it is hot enough, and then we will put in the bread;" but she intended when Gretel got in to shut up the oven and let her bake, so that she might eat her as well as Hansel. Gretel guessed what her thoughts were, and said, "I do not know how to do it; how shall I get in?" "You stupid goose," said she, "the opening is big enough. See, I could even get in myself!" and she got up and put her head into the oven. Then Gretel gave her a push, so that the witch fell right in, and then shutting the iron door she bolted it. Oh! how horribly the witch howled; but Gretel ran away, and left her to burn to ashes.

Now she ran to Hansel, and, opening his door, called out, "Hansel, we are saved; the old witch is dead!" So he sprang out, like a bird out of his cage when the door is opened. "We must be off now," said Hansel, "and get out of this bewitched forest."

When they had gone a little way, they came to a well-known wood and at last they saw their father's house. They began to run, and, bursting into the house, they ran to their father and hugged him. He had not had one happy hour since he had left the children in the forest. Then all their sorrows were ended, and they lived in great happiness.

Ha! Supper! What about my supper? I will fix you, Prince! No one ever worries about my supper. Your bit will be my bite. She looks delicious!

The Dragon's Mountain

This is the prophecy...A prince from afar will toast the dragon in his own fire to save his kin and the mountain will never again rumble.

The following instructions tell how to make the gingerbread characters in an original fairy-tale play for 4 marionettes. They are: the Prince, his friend Harlequin, his love the Princess, and a Dragon that lives in the mountain. The play, entitled "The Dragon's Mountain," comes after the instructions. At the end of the play, the terrible Dragon is turned into gingerbread by Harlequin. At that point, the hostess can pass around a plate full of gingerbread cookies shaped like dragons (see cookie patterns) so the young members of the audience can eat up their own gingerbread dragons too.

YOU WILL NEED:

1 batch Light Gingerbread Dough
1 batch Dark Gingerbread Dough
1 batch Royal Icing; Flow Frosting

1 egg white
Silver dragees

Heavy-duty brown or black carpet thread

MAKING THE PATTERNS

Make tracing paper and cardboard patterns for the marionettes and the dragon cookies following instructions in Basic Skills chapter.

MIXING THE DOUGH

Prepare 1 batch each of Light Gingerbread Dough and Dark Gingerbread Dough following recipes in Games chapter.

CUTTING

You will be preparing 5 cookie sheets (4 for the marionettes and 1 for the dragon cookies), but you can probably bake only 2 at a time. So after you roll out all the dough on foil or waxed paper, you can slide it onto pieces of cardboard or large trays to refrigerate, and then transfer to cookie sheets after the first baking is done.

1. Divide both light and dark doughs in half, giving you 4 balls of dough.
2. One by one, place each ball between 2 pieces of aluminum foil or waxed paper and roll out to a 10 x 6-inch rectangle ⅛-inch in thickness.

3. Place foil or waxed paper rectangles on cookie sheets (or cardboard or trays) and chill for 15 minutes in freezer or 45 minutes in refrigerator, or until firm.
4. Remove foil-covered dough from cookie sheets and set on work surface, then remove top pieces of foil or waxed paper from dough.
5. Position cardboard patterns on dough. Cut out pieces following instructions in Basic Skills chapter.

Note: refer to the chart which lists each piece and tells you how many of each to cut out of which color dough.

6. After cutting Harlequin's sleeves and jacket from dark dough, cut out upper neck and bottom of sleeve from light dough.
7. Set aside ¼ teaspoon of light dough for dragon's eye, then knead together the scraps of light and then the dark dough, making 2 balls. Refrigerate until ready to make dragon cookies.
8. After you have baked and decorated the marionettes, roll out the 2 reserve balls of dough one at a time and cut out and bake dragon cookies to serve your guests after the performance.

ASSEMBLING THE DRAGON

1. Cover a cookie sheet about 16 x 14 inches with lightly oiled foil.
2. Stir the egg white a bit.
3. Position 1 of each of the 3 dragon body pieces on the foil ⅛-inch apart. Put 1 flame piece inside but not touching dragon's mouth. The color photographs show how the pieces go together.

Note: carefully slide or peel cut-out pieces from foil or waxed paper backing before easing onto cookie sheets.

4. Brush pieces lightly with beaten egg white.
5. Measure and cut 3 pieces of thread slightly shorter than the length of the dragon, then position threads lengthwise on dragon, 1 inch apart.
6. Position 3 short pieces of thread crosswise to attach flame to mouth.
7. Cut four 24-inch lengths of thread, tie a loop in the end of each, and place on dragon.

8. Brush dragon again with egg white.
9. Carefully position 3 duplicate pieces of dragon body and 1 flame piece on top of string and pieces on cookie sheet, then press the 2 layers of dough together.
10. To mark design details, position corresponding tracing paper pattern over each dragon piece and make pinpricks through the paper into the dough. See Basic Skills chapter for instructions.

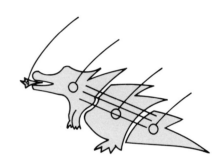

ASSEMBLING THE PRINCESS

1. Follow general instructions for assembling dragon. Position pieces on foil-covered cookie sheet, using the color photographs as your guide, and brush with egg white.
2. Measure, cut, and position on Princess lengths of thread long enough to attach blouse to skirt pieces and shoes.
3. Measure, cut, and position 1 piece of thread to run from left hand and arm over blouse to right arm and hand.
4. Cut two 48-inch pieces of thread. Fold in half, tie loop in folded end, and position to make strings for hands and feet.
5. Measure and cut a 24-inch piece of thread, tie loop in 1 end, position on blouse, and run through head to make main string for Princess.
6. Brush Princess again with egg white.
7. Position duplicate top pieces over strings, press layers together, and mark design details following tracing paper patterns.

ASSEMBLING THE PRINCE

Follow general instructions for assembling dragon and Princess.

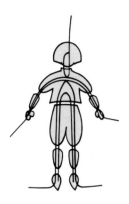

ASSEMBLING THE HARLEQUIN

1. Again follow general instructions for assembling the other marionettes.
2. But when positioning duplicate top pieces over strings, use light dough pieces for upper neck, collar pieces, sleeve bottoms, and sleeve ruffles. You can use the color photographs as your guide.
3. Press layers together and mark design details as for other marionettes.

BAKING

1. Bake marionettes, 2 cookie sheets at a time if you wish, at 350°F for 12 to 15 minutes or until dough feels firm to the touch.
2. Cool for 5 minutes, then gently test the movement of the puppets' sections. Using a sharp, pointed knife, carefully cut away any pieces of gingerbread that have expanded so sections don't move freely.
3. Cool cookie sheets completely, then carefully remove puppets from foil.
4. Bake dragon cookies for same time at same temperature, then cool completely and remove from foil.

DECORATING

1. Prepare Royal Icing following instructions in Basic Skills chapter, but before icing becomes stiff, put 1 heaping·tablespoon of it into each of 4 small bowls for Flow Frosting mixture. Cover bowls tightly with plastic wrap.
2. Beat remaining icing until stiff.
3. Attach writing tip to pastry bag or parchment cone, fill with white icing, and outline the design details marked on the dough. Use the color photographs as a guide as well. Allow icing to dry completely before applying Flow Frosting.
4. Mix red, blue, green, and yellow Flow Frostings in small bowls following instructions in Basic Skills chapter.
5. Color marionettes with Flow Frostings following instructions in Basic Skills chapter. You can use the photographs as your color guide, or decorate to suit your own fancy.
6. Ice silver dragee decorations on marionettes as shown in photographs.
7. Allow Flow Frosting to dry completely.

FINISHING TOUCHES

1. Cut a piece of cardboard into six ½ x 5-inch strips.
2. One at a time, tape 2 strips together, making 3 Xs.
3. Punch holes in ends of 3 Xs and attach to strings of Princess, Prince, and Harlequin.
4. Cut one ½ x 10-inch strip of cardboard, punch holes in both ends, and attach dragon's strings.

Pattern pieces	Dough	Cut
Dragon's head	dark	2
middle	dark	2
tail	dark	2
flame	light	2
Princess' skirt	light	2
blouse	light	2
head	light	2
arm	light	4
hand	light	4
shoe	dark	4
Prince's head	light	2
jacket	light	2
arm	light	4
pants	dark	2
legs	dark	4
Harlequin's head	dark	2
jacket	dark	2
pants	dark	2
sleeve	dark	4
legs	dark	4
face	dark	1
	light	1
Harlequin's ruffles	dark	2
	light	2
Harlequin's collar	dark	2
	light	2
Hand (Prince and Harlequin)	light	8
Shoes (Prince and Harlequin)	dark	8

121

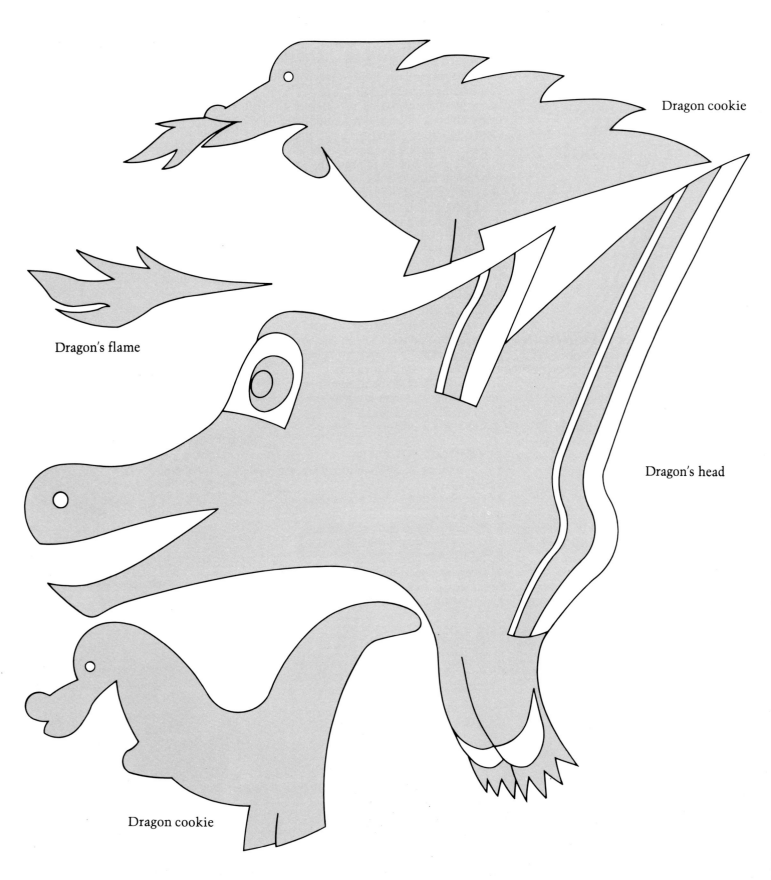

Dragon cookie

Dragon's flame

Dragon's head

Dragon cookie

122

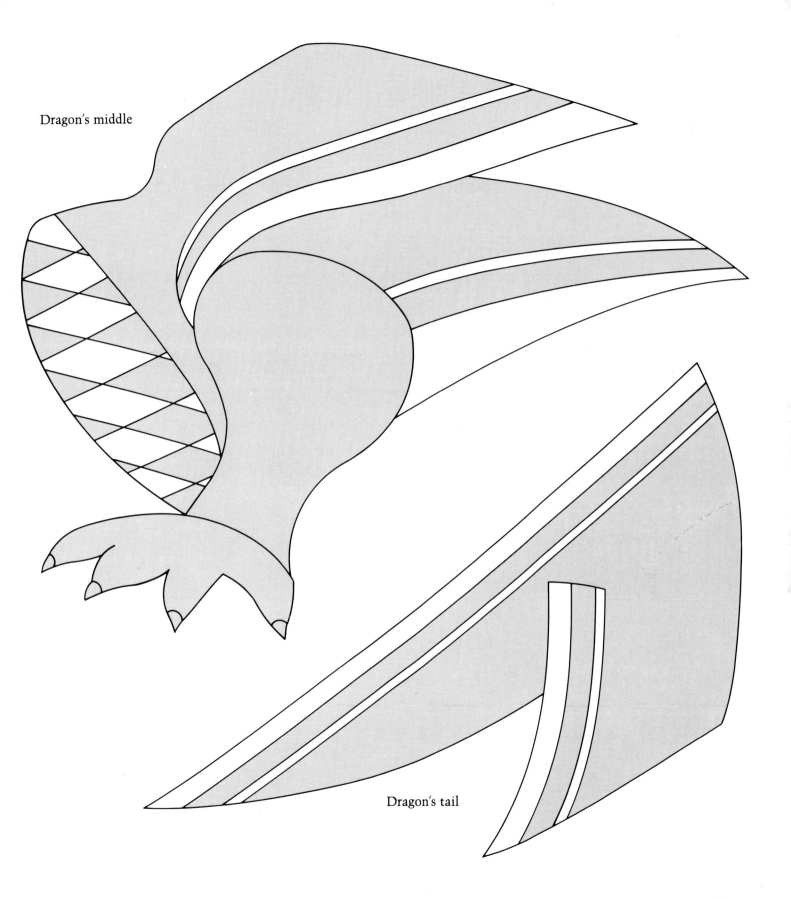

Dragon's middle

Dragon's tail

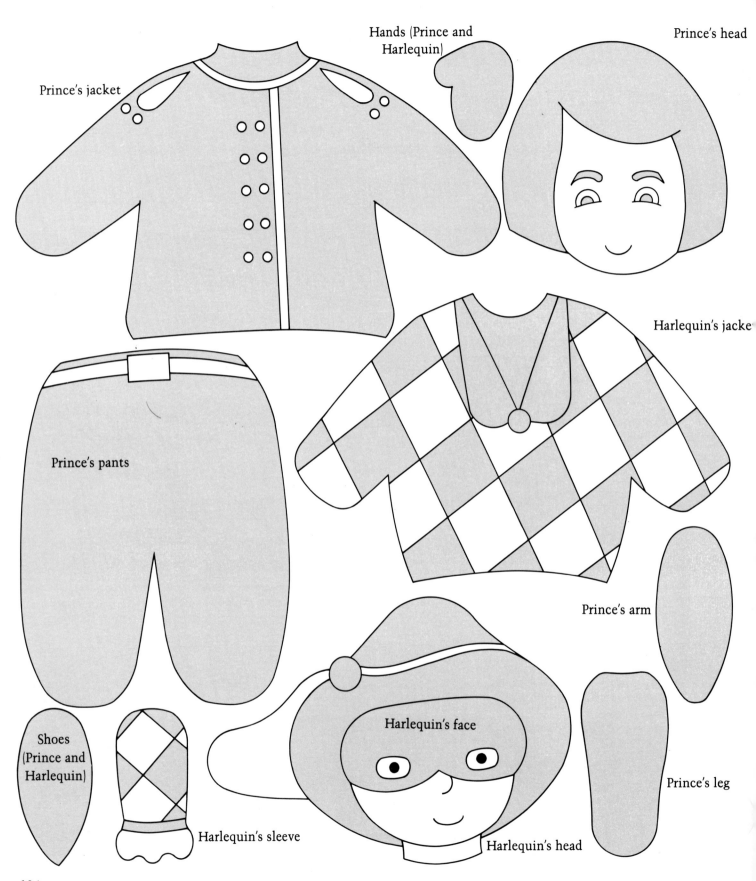

Hands (Prince and Harlequin)

Prince's head

Prince's jacket

Harlequin's jacke

Prince's pants

Prince's arm

Shoes (Prince and Harlequin)

Harlequin's face

Prince's leg

Harlequin's sleeve

Harlequin's head

Princess' head

Princess' blouse

Princess' hand

Princess' arm

Princess' skirt

Harlequin's pants

Harlequin's leg

Princess' shoe

THE DRAGON MUST DIE
A Fairy Tale Play in Three Scenes

SCENE I — *The Seaside near the Palace*

NARRATOR: Once upon a time there was a tiny kingdom snuggled into the side of a great mountain. As we come upon our little kingdom, there is great excitement, for today a beautiful Princess is to arrive from afar to marry the Prince. Just a moment! Her boat is entering the harbor now.

[Enter Prince and Harlequin.]

PRINCE: My Princess has arrived. I am so happy. I am so nervous. Say something, my friend; you always know what to say. Will she be happy? How can she be happy here? Do you think the legend of our mountain has traveled across the sea?

HARLEQUIN: You ask too many questions, my friend, my very best friend. If you are happy, she will be happy. Here, have a muffin with me. That will make me happy.

PRINCE: I'm not hungry. Here she comes. Isn't she beautiful!

HARLEQUIN: Go meet your Princess. I will have my two beautiful muffins.

[Enter Princess. Exit Harlequin.]

PRINCESS: My Prince (offers hand).

PRINCE: Welcome to my kingdom, your new home. We are all so happy you have come. I would like you to meet my very best friend (Looks for Harlequin). Now where did he go? Well, let us go to the palace. I am sure we will find him at supper.

[Exit Prince and Princess. Enter Dragon.]

DRAGON: Ha! Supper! What about my supper? I will fix you, Prince! No one ever worries about my supper. Your bit will be my bite. She looks delicious!

[Exit Dragon. Enter Harlequin stealthily.]

HARLEQUIN: How inconvenient! That dragon pops up at the worst times. I knew the rumbling had started. I must warn my s..., the Princess.

[Exit Harlequin.]

SCENE II — *The Garden*

[Enter Princess.]

PRINCESS: (nervously) What a beautiful garden. I just can't sleep tonight; I will stay here awhile. What was that? I wonder why the ground rumbles so? Why am I so unhappy on the eve of my wedding? The Prince seems so nice and the kingdom is so beautiful, but the people do not seem very happy. I miss my father, my dear father. If only I could have stayed with him. He is so lonely now that my brother is gone and it is such a burden for him to run the kingdom all by himself. If only the pirates had not taken my brother; if only he would come back, everything would be all right.

[Enter Harlequin.]

HARLEQUIN: Don't be afraid Princess, I am a friend. I will keep you company. Why are you so unhappy? My Prince, my very best friend, wants so much for you to be happy here.

PRINCESS: Oh, Harlequin, I want so much to be happy here too, but I miss my dear father whom I have left all alone in my homeland. And things are not at all as I had expected them to be here. Everything is so beautiful, but no one seems to be very happy. And why does the ground shake so?

HARLEQUIN: My Princess, you remind me so much of the sister I left behind when pirates took me from my homeland. I too have sorrows, however, I will try to entertain you. But first, I have come to warn you! There is something you must know. You must know the legend. The legend will answer all your questions.

PRINCESS: Oh thank you for helping me. I know you are my friend, I feel as if I have known you in another life.

HARLEQUIN: Now, the legend: although no one now alive has seen it happen, legend has it that there is a great fire inside the beautiful mountain. The dragon who lives at the top of the mountain is master of the Fire and when he commands it to do so, it spills from its home in the center of the mountain and destroys all in its path. It is the dragon poking up his great fire that makes the ground rumble and shake. The people are very unhappy because the rumbling means that the dragon is about to punish the village again. For long periods of time, the mountain is very quiet and the people begin to enjoy their peaceful lives and the beautiful countryside. Then the rumbling starts and soon a young woman disappears from the village never to be seen again.

PRINCESS: Oh, how terrible!

HARLEQUIN: Although I have only been here a few years, I have seen it happen twice before. Would you like a cookie? All this talking has made me quite hungry.

PRINCESS: Not now, please go on with the story.

HARLEQUIN: That is the legend; as soon as I finish this cookie I will tell you the prophecy. Would you like to share a cupcake? Cook made some delicious cupcakes today.

PRINCESS: Please go on!

HARLEQUIN: The prophecy is [munch, munch,] although the people live in fear of the dragon and his mountain, there is a hope, the prophecy. In the royal library, there is a document. No one knows how it got there, for it has been there longer than anyone can remember. Whenever the rumbling starts and someone disappears, the King reads it to the people to remind them that there is a hope. This is the prophecy.... A Prince from afar will toast the dragon in his own fire to save his kin and the mountain will never again rumble.

PRINCESS: How do you know there is a dragon? I don't believe in dragons.

HARLEQUIN: Neither did I until I saw him. I have seen this dragon this very day, Princess, and you are his intended victim. You must be very careful. And now I will entertain you with a happy story. But what is that noise?

[Harlequin turns around and Dragon snatches Princess.]

DRAGON: Now I have you, my beauty, you are mine! Doesn't she look delicious, Harlequin? She will be a feast you could appreciate.

HARLEQUIN: [hitting dragon] No, no, put her down.

[Dragon pushes Harlequin down and runs off with the Princess.]

SCENE III — *The Mountain*

DRAGON: Ah hah! The fire is almost ready for toasting. You will make such a good supper.

PRINCESS: No, no, I won't be at all delicious. I am very unhappy; I will not be delicious at all.

DRAGON: Just let me look at that fire again.

[Harlequin pops out, kicks the Dragon into the fire with his foot, hugs Princess.]

HARLEQUIN: You are my long lost sister; you must be my sister. I have felt it since I first saw you.

PRINCESS: Oh yes, and you are my brother who was taken away by the pirates. I am so happy; our father will be so happy! But how did you get here?

HARLEQUIN: After the pirates took me from our father's palace, we sailed around the world stopping ships for their gold and raiding small towns for their treasures. Then one day a great storm hit our boat and the next thing I knew, I was on the beach where your boat landed today. The Prince found me and was so delighted by my company that he has allowed me to stay here and live in the palace. But now we must get you back to the palace. The Prince will soon discover you are missing and be upset. Let's not forget the dragon; he smells delicious, and I'm just getting hungry.

[Back at the Palace]

PRINCE: My Princess, what has happened?

HARLEQUIN: There is no time for that now—on with the wedding, and wait until you see the delicious gingerbread dragon we have brought for the feast. I get the ears!

NARRATOR: After the wedding, the townspeople enjoyed the dragon feast. Harlequin went back to his homeland to assume his rightful position and to help his father rule the kingdom. The Prince and Princess visited often and they all lived happily ever after.

THE END

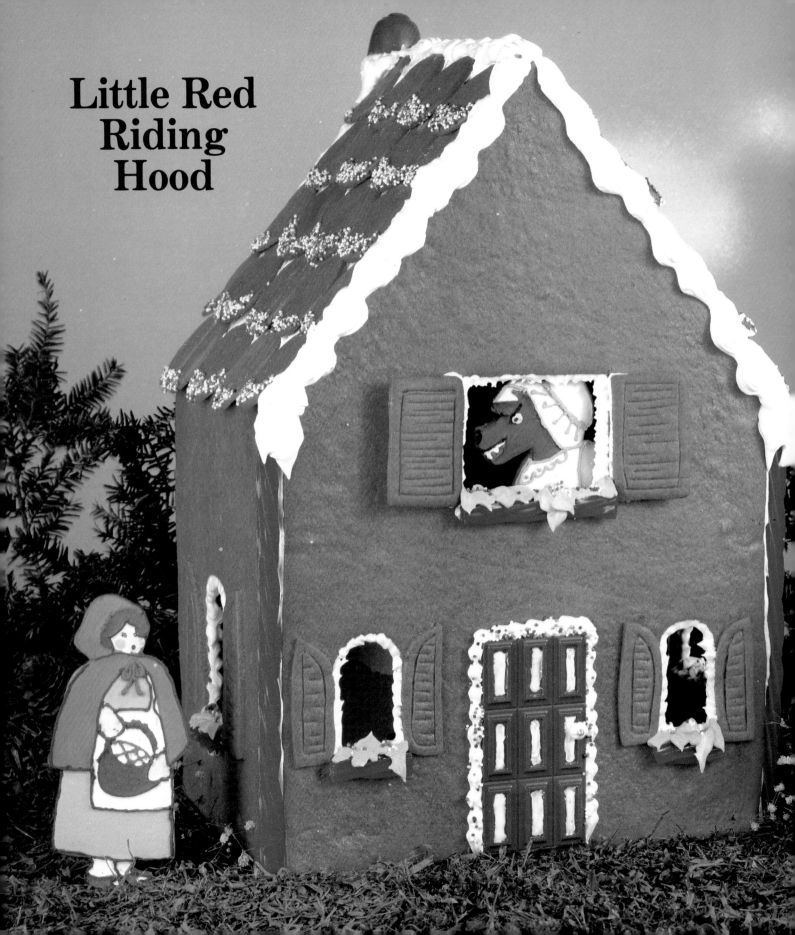

Little Red
Riding
Hood

Although the three bears, Goldilocks, Little Red Riding Hood, Granny, and the Wolf didn't all live in the same house at the *same* time, let's pretend they might have at *different* times. This allows you to make only one house and change the setting to illustrate two different fairy tales. The house has a big front window with a platform inside so you can stand a cookie-character on it which will be seen through the window.

THREE LITTLE RED RIDING BEARS

One House with Three Bears, Goldilocks, Red Riding Hood, Granny, and the Wolf

YOU WILL NEED:

See Basic Skills chapter for general equipment and materials.

2 batches Dark Gingerbread Dough
1 batch Royal Icing; Flow Frosting
Food coloring for following tints: red, green, yellow, blue, and brown.

Edibles: 1 (1.45 ounce) milk chocolate bar; red licorice whips; multicolored candy shot; 1 chocolate-covered cherry; 1 silver dragee.

A stiff, flat base of ¼-inch plywood or heavy cardboard large enough to hold the entire scene. Or, you can use a spare metal tray.

In addition, have on hand: dull knife or spatula; masking tape; ¼-inch artist's brush; full food cans; corn syrup

MAKING THE PATTERNS

The evergreen tree patterns are shown in the Children's Village project full-sized. The patterns for house front/back and side are illustrated in reduced dimensions, accompanied by full-sized measurements. Use the full-sized color photographs as patterns for the fairy-tale figures.

1. Follow instructions in Basic Skills chapter for tracing and enlarging patterns, and for making cardboard patterns.
2. Cut out all window openings and reserve.

Note: be sure to make 2 cardboard house side patterns and 1 cardboard pattern each for house front and back. On the house back pattern, mark and cut out a 6-inch centered square opening instead of the windows shown on the reduced illustration. For this project, the thinly rolled dough is iced

to the corresponding cardboard pattern pieces before house is assembled and decorated.

3. Measure and cut the following cardboard patterns: one 10 x 8-inch rectangle for base; two 8-inch squares for roof pieces; and one 2-inch circle for roof tiles. (If you have a 2-inch round cookie cutter, use that to cut out the 40 tiles.)

See Basic Skills chapter for instructions on how to make supports for figures so they will stand upright.

MIXING THE DOUGH

Prepare 2 batches of Dark Gingerbread Dough following recipe in Games chapter.

CUTTING AND BAKING THE HOUSE PIECES

Roll out and cut only ½ a batch of dough (enough for 1 cookie sheet) at a time to prevent thinly rolled dough from drying out. Wrap reserve in plastic wrap and refrigerate.

1. Roll out dough on oiled, foil-lined cookie sheets following instructions in Basic Skills chapter, but roll to a thickness of ⅛ inch rather than ¼ inch.
2. Cut out cookie pieces for house following instructions in Basic Skills chapter. Cut 4 of the roof tiles in half.

Do not cut a base piece out of dough, but reserve this as well as all cardboard pattern pieces to use in assembling the house.

3. Shutters for house front and side windows are made from dough cutouts. Remove cutouts carefully with spatula and chill for a few minutes if dough is too soft. To make shutters for house sides and lower front windows, divide cutouts in half lengthwise. With a dull knife or spatula, score designs as shown in color photographs. Then moisten backs of cutouts with water and attach to house.

Note: do not attach shutters for upper front window. Cut these in half lengthwise, score, and place at edge of cookie sheet for baking.

4. Bake at 350°F for 6 to 8 minutes or

until cookie pieces are firm and lightly browned. Place cookie sheets on racks and cool completely before removing cookie pieces from foil.

CUTTING AND BAKING THE FIGURES

1. Roll out dough to ¼-inch thickness on oiled, foil-lined cookie sheet, and cut out figures and mark design details following instructions in Basic Skills chapter.
2. Bake at 350°F for 12 to 15 minutes or until cookie pieces are firm and lightly browned.
3. Cool cookie sheet on rack completely before removing pieces from foil.

ASSEMBLING THE CARDBOARD HOUSE FRAME

1. Lay front on flat surface. Place 1 house side on each side of front and secure with masking tape.
2. Cut a 3 x 2-inch rectangle of cardboard. Fold in half lengthwise and tape to inside of front several inches below upper window as a platform on which to place a fairy-tale figure.
3. Tape house back to 1 house side, tape roof pieces to tops of side pieces, and tape base at bottom of house front.
4. Life sides and back up and tape together to form a box, then lift base and tape to sides and back.
5. Set house on cardboard base. Fold roof pieces over and tape securely into place.

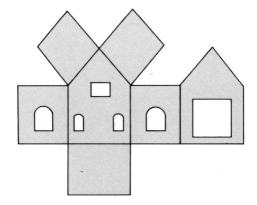

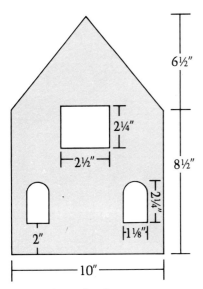

6½"

2¼"

2½"

8½"

2¼"

2"

1⅛"

10"

House front, back

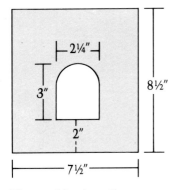

2¼"

3"

8½"

2"

7½"

House sides (cut 2)

ASSEMBLING THE HOUSE

1. Prepare 1 batch of Royal Icing following instructions in Basic Skills chapter. Reserve half of icing before it becomes stiff. You will use it later for Flow Frosting. Beat remaining icing until stiff, then cover tightly. Make a second batch of icing if you need it.

2. Spread a thin layer of white icing over cardboard house back and press cookie back piece into place. Allow to set. See Basic Skills chapter for instructions on applying Royal Icing.

3. Lay house on its back and repeat procedure with cookie side and front pieces. Allow to set. Prop with full food cans if necessary.

4. Spread a line of icing about ¼-inch thick along both sides of upper front window, and another line, slightly thicker, about ½ inch from first line. Press reserved shutter cutouts in position, leaning slightly away from house and resting on thicker line of frosting. Prop shutters, using pencils for support until they are dry.

5. Carefully trim 3 rows of chocolate from chocolate bar, spread thin layer of icing on 1 side, and position on center of house front to make door. Allow to dry completely.

DECORATING

1. Decorate evergreen trees and fairy-tale figures with Royal Icing and Flow Frosting. See Basic Skills chapter for instructions on tinting and applying icing and frosting. Use color photographs as guides, or decorate to suit your fancy.

2. Using a pastry bag or parchment cone fitted with a small star tip, pipe white icing borders around and inside windows. Allow to dry completely.

3. Lay house on its back, change to a large star tip, and pipe a row of white icing down each front corner and under each front window. Cut strips of red

licorice to fit and press into icing for trimming and to make window boxes. Allow to dry.

4. Set house upright. With large star tip, pipe a row of icing under each side window and press licorice in place to make more window boxes. Let dry completely.

5. Brush bottoms of roof tile pieces with corn syrup, then dip gently into multicolored candy shot. Allow to dry completely. Spread white icing on 1 side of roof, then press tiles in place, using color photographs as guides. Repeat for other side of roof. Allow to dry completely.

6. Using large star tip, pipe white icing around front edge of roof, making a series of stars or a shell border. Follow instructions in House of Cats chapter. Pipe border along roof ridge, adding a large puff of icing at back. Press chocolate-covered cherry into puff for chimney. Let dry completely.

7. Pipe white icing border around front door and sprinkle with multicolored candy shot. Pipe a dot for door knob and press silver dragee into it. Let dry completely.

8. Using leaf tip, frost leaves onto window boxes, then sprinkle with multicolored candy shot.

9. Let house and trees dry at least 4 hours or overnight before moving.

FINISHING TOUCHES

To make a charming centerpiece, cover base with artificial grass and place house on it. For Little Red Riding Hood and her friends, surround house with real evergreen boughs and pine cones to simulate a forest. Or put up a white picket fence and add a branch or two of real flowers for Goldilocks and the Three Bears.

Attach supports to backs of fairy-tale figures with icing following instructions in Basic Skills chapter. Arrange as shown in photographs.

Use the full-sized color photographs as patterns for the fairy-tale figures.

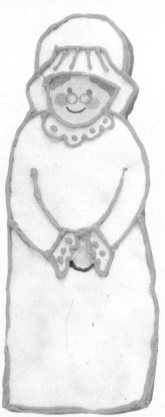

Granny, waiting
for Little Red Riding
Hood to arrive

Noble, fearless woodsman

"Why, bless my stars;
Me? A wolf?"

Little Red Riding Hood,
her very self

"Yummy," said Goldilocks

Gretel broke off a piece
of the roof

"Strawberry Licorice," said
Hansel with his mouth ful

Use the full-sized color photographs
as patterns for the fairy-tale figures.

Poppa Bear, Baby Bear,
and Mamma Bear returning home

This one is looking
for a pig in a house of sticks

"I'll huff and I'll puff,
and I'll blow
away your shredded wheat."

"Couldn't budge the bricks,
so it's down the chimney."

"Who's munching
my mansion!"

The Story
of the
Three
Bears

ONCE UPON A TIME there were Three Bears, who lived together in a house of their own, in a wood. One of them was a Little, Small, Wee Bear; and one was a Middle-sized Bear, and the other was a Great, Huge Bear.

One day, after they had made the porridge for their breakfast, they walked out into the wood to give it time to cool. And while they were out who do you think came to their door but a tired, hungry little girl named... Goldilocks. She looked in the window, and seeing nobody in the house, she lifted the latch and went in. And well pleased she was to see the porridge on the table.

First she tasted the porridge of the Great, Huge Bear, and that was too hot. Then she tasted the porridge of the Middle-sized Bear, and that was too cold. Then she tasted the porridge of the Small, Wee Bear, and that was neither too hot nor too cold but just right, so she ate it all up.

Then she looked for a chair to sit upon. First she tried the chair of the Great, Huge Bear, and that was too hard. Then she tried the chair of the Middle-sized Bear, and that was too soft. Then she tried the chair of the Small, Wee Bear, and that was neither too hard nor too soft but just right, so there she sat and would have fallen asleep, but the bottom of the chair came out, and down she came, plump upon the floor.

Goldilocks was so sleepy that she didn't cry at all but picked herself up, and went upstairs to the bedchamber where the Three Bears slept. First she lay down on the bed of the Great, Huge Bear and that was too high. Then she lay down on the bed of the Middle-sized Bear and that was too low. Then she lay down on the bed of the Small, Wee Bear, and that was neither too high nor too low, but just right, so she covered herself up and fell fast asleep.

By this time the Three Bears thought their porridge would be cool enough, so they came home to breakfast. Now Goldilocks had forgotten to close and latch the door, and the Bears knew immediately that someone was in their house. First they went to the table.

"Somebody's been eating my porridge!"

said the Great, Huge Bear, in his great, rough voice.

"Somebody's been eating my porridge!"

said the Middle-sized Bear in her middle-sized voice.

"Somebody's been eating my porridge, and has eaten it all up!"

said the Little, Small, Wee Bear, in his little, small wee voice.

Then they looked about them and saw that their chairs were out of place.

"Somebody's been sitting in my chair!"

said the Great, Huge Bear, in his great, rough voice.

"Somebody's been sitting in my chair!"

said the Middle-sized Bear in her middle-sized voice.

Then the Little, Small, Wee Bear looked at his chair and saw that it was broken.

"Somebody's been sitting in my chair and has sat the bottom out of it!"

said the Little, Small, Wee Bear, in his little, small, wee voice.

Then the Three Bears thought they should make further search; so they went upstairs into their bedchamber. Now the Great Huge Bear didn't have a chance to say anything in his great, huge voice; and the Middle-sized Bear didn't have a chance to say anything in her middle-sized voice, because the Little, Small, Wee Bear had already seen Goldilocks fast asleep in his bed.

"Here is the somebody who has been eating our porridge, and sitting in our chairs, and sleeping in our beds; and she looks very nice; and I'm sure she was just very hungry, and tired, and sleepy, and can we keep her please?"

said the Little, Small, Wee Bear in his small, wee, and very excited voice.

And the Great, Huge Bear and the Middle-sized Bear said yes they could keep her if the little girl wanted to stay. So they woke her up, and she did, so they did, and they lived happily ever after.

The Story of the Three Little Pigs

Once upon a time when pigs spoke rhyme
And monkeys chewed tobacco,
And hens took snuff to make them tough,
And ducks went quack, quack, quack, O!

THERE was an old sow with three little pigs, and as she had not enough to keep them, she sent them out to seek their fortune. The first that went off met a man with a bundle of straw, and said to him:

"Please, man, give me that straw to build me a house."

Which the man did, and the little pig built a house with it. Presently came along a wolf, and knocked at the door, and said:

"Little pig, little pig, let me come in."

To which the pig answered:

"No, no, by the hair of my chiny chin chin."

The wolf then answered to that:

"Then I'll huff, and I'll puff, and I'll blow your house in."

So he huffed, and he puffed, and he blew his house in, and ate up the little pig.

The second little pig met a man with a bundle of furze and said:

"Please, man, give me that furze to build a house."

Which the man did, and the pig built his house. Then along came the wolf, and said:

"Little pig, little pig, let me come in."

"No, no, by the hair of my chiny chin chin."

"Then I'll puff, and I'll huff, and I'll blow your house in."

So he huffed, and he puffed, and he puffed, and he huffed, and at last he blew the house down, and he ate up the little pig.

The third little pig met a man with a load of bricks, and said:

"Please, man, give me those bricks to build a house with."

So the man gave him the bricks, and he built his house with them. So the wolf came, as he did to the other little pigs, and said:

"Little pig, little pig, let me come in."

"No, no, by the hair on my chiny chin chin."

"Then I'll huff, and I'll puff, and I'll blow your house in."

Well, he huffed, and he puffed, and he huffed and he puffed, and he puffed and huffed; but he could *not* get the house down. When he found that he could not, with all his huffing and puffing, blow the house down, he said:

"Little pig, I know where there is a nice field of turnips."

"Where?" said the little pig.

"Oh, in Mr. Smith's Home-field, and if you will be ready to-morrow morning I will call for you, and we will go together, and get some for dinner."

"Very well," said the little pig, "I will be ready. What time do you mean to go?"

"Oh, at six o'clock."

Well, the little pig got up at five, and got the turnips before the wolf came (which he did about six), who said:

"Little pig, are you ready?"

The little pig said: "Ready! I have been and come back again, and got a nice potful for dinner."

The wolf felt very angry at this, but thought that he would be up to the little pig somehow or other, so he said:

"Little pig, I know where there is a nice appletree."

"Where?" said the pig.

"Down at Merry-garden," replied the wolf, "and if you will not deceive me I will come for you at five o'clock to-morrow and get some apples."

Well, the little pig bustled up the next morning at four o'clock, and went off for the apples, hoping to get back before the wolf came; but he had further to go, and had to climb the tree, so that just as he was coming down from it, he saw the wolf coming, which, as you may suppose, frightened him very much. When the wolf came up he said:

"Little pig, what! are you here before me? Are they nice apples?"

"Yes, very," said the little pig. "I will throw you down one."

And he threw it so far, that, while the wolf was gone to pick it up, the little pig jumped down and ran home. The next day the wolf came again, and said to the little pig:

"Little pig, there is a fair at Shanklin this afternoon, will you go?"

"Oh yes," said the pig, "I will go; what time shall you be ready?"

"At three," said the wolf. So the little pig went off before the time as usual, and got to the fair, and bought a butter-churn, which he was going home with, when he saw the wolf coming. Then he could not tell what to do. So he got into the churn to hide, and by so doing turned it round, and it rolled down the hill with the pig in it, which frightened the wolf so much, that he ran home without going to the fair. He went to the little pig's house, and told him how frightened he had been by a great round thing which came down the hill past him. Then the little pig said:

"Hah, I frightened you, then. I had been to the fair and bought a butter-churn, and when I saw you, I got into it, and rolled down the hill."

Then the wolf was very angry indeed, and declared he *would* eat up the little pig, and that he would get down the chimney after him. When the little pig saw what he was about, he hung on the pot full of water, and made up a blazing fire, and, just as the wolf was coming down, took off the cover, and in fell the wolf; so the little pig put on the cover again in an instant, boiled him up, and ate him for supper, and lived happy ever afterwards.

Little Red Riding Hood

ONCE UPON A TIME there was a little village girl, the prettiest that had ever been seen. Her mother doted on her. Her grandmother was even fonder, and made her a little red hood, which became her so well that everywhere she went by the name of Little Red Riding Hood.

One day her mother, who had just made and baked some cakes, said to her:

"Go and see how your grandmother is, for I have been told that she is ill. Take her a cake and this little pot of butter."

Little Red Riding Hood set off at once for the house of her grandmother, who lived in another village.

On her way through a wood she met old Father Wolf. He would have very much liked to eat her, but dared not do so on account of some wood-cutters who were in the forest. He asked her where she was going. The poor child, not knowing that it was dangerous to stop and listen to a wolf, said:

"I am going to see my grandmother, and am taking her a cake and a pot of butter which my mother has sent to her."

"Does she live far away?" asked the Wolf.

"Oh, yes," replied Little Red Riding Hood; "it is yonder by the mill which you can see right below there, and it is the first house in the village."

"Well now," said the Wolf, "I think I shall go and see her too. I will go by this path, and you by that path, and we will see who gets there first."

The Wolf set off running with all his might by the shorter road, and the little girl continued on her way by the longer road. As she went she amused herself by gathering nuts, running after the butterflies, and making nosegays of the wild flowers which she found.

The Wolf was not long in reaching the grandmother's house.

He knocked. *Toc Toc.*

"Who is there?"

"It is your granddaughter, Red Riding Hood," said the Wolf, disguising his voice, "and I bring you a cake and a little pot of butter as a present from my mother."

The worthy grandmother was in bed, not being very well, and cried out to him:

"Pull out the peg and the latch will fall."

The Wolf drew out the peg and the door flew open. Then he sprang upon the poor old lady and ate her up in less than no time, for he had been more than three days without food.

After that he shut the door, lay down in the grandmother's bed, and waited for Little Red Riding Hood.

Presently she came and knocked. *Toc Toc.*

"Who is there?"

Now Little Red Riding Hood on hearing the Wolf's gruff voice was at first frightened, but thinking that her grandmother had a bad cold, she replied:

"It is your granddaughter, Red Riding Hood, and I bring you a cake and a little pot of butter from my mother."

Softening his voice, the Wolf called out to her:

"Pull out the peg and the latch will fall."

Little Red Riding Hood drew out the peg and the door flew open.

When he saw her enter, the Wolf hid himself in the bed beneath the counterpane.

"Put the cake and the little pot of butter on the bin," he said, "and come up on the bed with me."

Little Red Riding Hood took off her cloak, but when she climbed up on the bed she was astonished to see how her grandmother looked in her nightgown.

"Grandmother dear!" she exclaimed, "what big arms you have!"

"The better to embrace you, my child!"

"Grandmother dear, what big legs you have!"

"The better to run with, my child!"

"Grandmother dear, what big ears you have!"

"The better to hear with, my child!"

"Grandmother dear, what big eyes you have!"

"The better to see with, my child!"

"Grandmother dear, what big teeth you have!"

"The better to eat you with!"

With these words the wicked Wolf leapt upon Little Red Riding Hood and gobbled her up.

In the story of the Three Little Pigs, "furze" is a spiney shrub, sometimes called "gorse," that grows in Europe. "Sticks" is close enough to "furze" in meaning to be substituted if you like.

Three Little Pigs

"Once upon a time...", but you know the story. One house was made of bricks (wolf will *never* fit down that chimney), another was made of sticks (has the wolf found an open window?), and the third was made of straw (with a shredded wheat thatch that's about to be blown away).

Make tracing paper and cardboard patterns of the two pigs that are shown full size on facing page. Follow instructions in Basic Skills chapter. Use side-view pattern twice as follows. Cut 1 cookie, then flour cardboard lightly and turn it over to make pig facing in other direction. For the three wolves, use as patterns the full-color photo following Little Red Riding Hood project, p. 133.

YOU WILL NEED:
See Basic Skills chapter for general equipment and materials.

1 batch Basic Corn Syrup Gingerbread Dough
1 batch Royal Icing; Flow Frosting Food colorings to mix tints of red, pink, yellow, turquoise, green, and brown

Edibles: Shredded wheat; pretzel sticks; silver dragees; brown, tan, yellow, and orange chocolate-filled candies; yellow and green candy buttons; nonpareils; cinnamon hots; spearmint leaves; green sprinkles

Stiff, flat base of ¼-inch plywood or heavy cardboard large enough to hold houses and figures. Or, you can use a spare metal tray.

MAKING THE PATTERNS
All 3 houses are made from the same basic patterns, which are illustrated in reduced dimensions, accompanied by full-sized measurements. To make full-sized cardboard patterns, follow instructions in Basic Skills chapter. Follow same instructions for making patterns for Stick House shed and Brick House chimney.

Make tracing paper and cardboard patterns for pigs and wolves, which are shown full size, following instructions in Basic Skills chapter. 2 pigs are shown from opposite side views. When you have cut cookie piece from cardboard pattern positioned on 1 side, turn pattern over, flour lightly, and cut cookie piece facing in opposite direction.

MIXING THE DOUGH
Mix 1 batch Basic Corn Syrup

Gingerbread Dough following instructions in Basic Skills chapter.

CUTTING AND BAKING
Cut out cookie pieces, mark design details, and bake following instructions in Basic Skills chapter.

DECORATING THE FIGURES
1. Make 1 batch of Royal Icing and mix Flow Frosting following instructions in Basic Skills chapter. Reserve 2 tablespoons of icing in each of 6 small bowls and mix red frosting and brown icing for Brick House, and pink, yellow, turquoise, green, and brown frosting for the 3 pigs and the wolves.
2. Decorate figures with Royal Icing and Flow Frosting using the color photograph as your guide and following instructions in Basic Skills chapter for applying icing and frosting.

DECORATING THE STRAW HOUSE
1. Using parchment cone or pastry bag, knife, or paintbrush, spread white Flow Frosting all over surface of house side, front, and back pieces. Do not frost roof. Quickly but gently press pieces of shredded wheat into frosting while it is still moist. Allow to set about 10 minutes.
2. Dot icing on candy buttons and decorate shutters, alternating green and yellow candies. Allow to dry completely, about 4 hours.
3. Pipe icing on undecorated side of each shutter and position on either side of open window. Hold in place until set, about 5 minutes, then allow to dry completely.
4. To decorate roof pieces, use pastry bag or parchment cone fitted with medium plain round tip. Pipe white icing lattice work, then, before icing sets, attach a silver dragee at each cross point. Use the color photograph as a decorating guide. Allow to dry completely.
5. Decorate door with white icing and yellow button candies and allow to dry completely. Don't forget the silver dragee doorknob.
6. Ice candy buttons around outside

edge of door opening, alternating yellow and green candies. Pipe icing along right side of door opening and attach door in open position. Allow to dry completely.

DECORATING THE STICK HOUSE
1. Spread white frosting over surfaces of house pieces as for Straw House, but instead of shredded wheat, press pretzel sticks into frosting. Allow to dry completely.
2. Decorate and attach shutters as for Straw House, but use cinnamon hots instead of green and yellow candies. Decorate front window with yellow candy buttons.
3. Decorate shed pieces with white icing, cinnamon hots, and green sprinkles, using color photograph as a guide.
4. Decorate door and outside edge of door opening with white icing, then attach door as for Straw House.

DECORATING THE BRICK HOUSE
1. Mix red frosting and spread over house pieces as for Straw House.
2. Carefully pipe on brick lines, using parchment cone or pastry bag fitted with small plain round tip and filled with brown icing.
3. To decorate roof, pipe white icing lattice work as for Straw House, then position cinnamon hots at each cross point.
4. Decorate shutters with white icing and attach as for Straw House.
5. Decorate chimney pieces and door with white icing, and outside edge of door with cinnamon hots. Attach door as for Straw House.

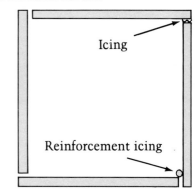

Icing

Reinforcement icing

ASSEMBLING THE HOUSES

1. The walls and roof for all 3 houses are assembled in the same way. See the Construction section in Basic Skills chapter for instructions on assembling the basic box shape.

2. To assemble Stick House shed, attach front, back, and side pieces with icing, then pipe icing along slanted tops of front and back pieces and position shed roof. Hold in place until set, then allow to dry completely. Pipe icing along shed sides and top and position against side of house. Hold in place until set, then let dry completely.

3. To assemble Brick House chimney, pipe icing along edges to join pieces, hold in place until set, then allow to dry completely. Ice bottom, slanted edge of chimney and position on right side of roof. Hold in place until set. Allow to dry completely.

4. After 3 houses are completely assembled, pipe white icing along top seams of roofs and position rows of candy decoration: brown and tan chocolate-filled candies for the Straw

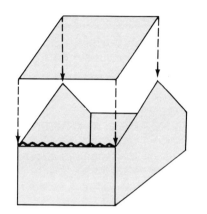

House; cinnamon hots for the Stick House; and yellow and orange chocolate-filled candies for the Brick House. Allow to dry completely.

FINISHING TOUCHES

1. Cover base with aluminum foil and spread white Flow Frosting over entire surface. Before frosting sets, cover with green sprinkles to make "grass."

2. Ice or just set 3 houses on base.

3. Ice wolf and pig figures to base, or, if you want to be able to move them around, see Basic Skills chapter for instructions on making stands for them. Ice wolves to Straw House shed and Brick House chimney.

4. Complete the scene with spearmint leaf bushes and pathways made of nonpareils iced to base.

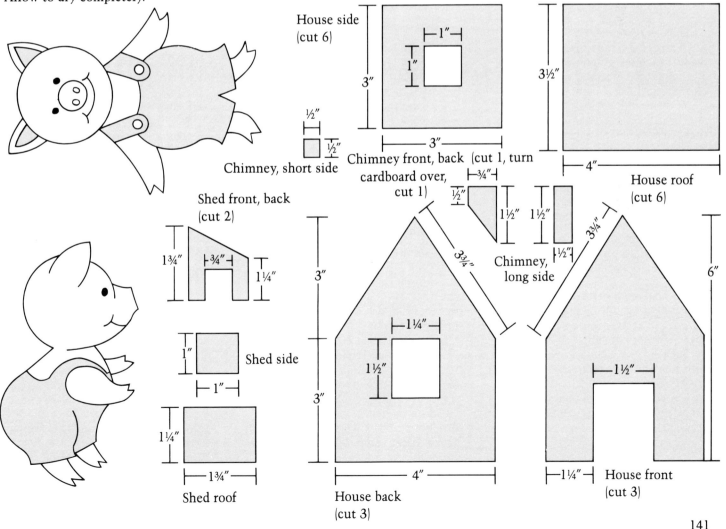

House side (cut 6)

Chimney, short side

Chimney front, back (cut 1, turn cardboard over, cut 1)

Chimney, long side

House roof (cut 6)

Shed front, back (cut 2)

Shed side

Shed roof

House back (cut 3)

House front (cut 3)

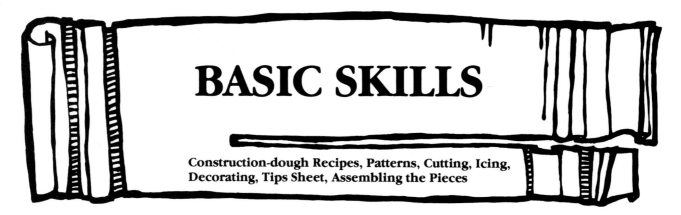

BASIC SKILLS

Construction-dough Recipes, Patterns, Cutting, Icing, Decorating, Tips Sheet, Assembling the Pieces

BASIC CORN SYRUP GINGERBREAD DOUGH

  9 cups unsifted flour
  1 tablespoon grated lemon rind
1½ tablespoons ground cinnamon
  1 tablespoon ground ginger
  ½ teaspoon salt
  2 cups light corn syrup
1½ cups firmly packed light brown
    sugar
1¼ cups butter or margarine

1. In large bowl, combine flour, lemon rind, cinnamon, ginger, and salt.
2. In 3-quart saucepan, stir together corn syrup, brown sugar, and butter. Cook over medium heat, stirring constantly, until butter is melted and ingredients are well mixed.
3. Pour liquid mixture into flour mixture and stir until well blended.

Note: check specific project directions for special rolling, cutting, and baking instructions before proceeding with this recipe.

4. Form dough into ball and knead until smooth and pliable.
5. Roll out dough on foil-lined cookie sheets to ¼-inch thickness, using lightly floured rolling pin.
6. Cut out cookie pieces, remove and reserve excess dough.
7. Bake in 350°F oven 12 to 15 minutes or until cookies are firm and lightly browned.
8. Cool cookie sheets completely on racks before removing cookie pieces from foil.

BASIC MOLASSES GINGERBREAD DOUGH

  8 cups unsifted flour
  2 teaspoons ground cinnamon
  2 teaspoons ground ginger
  2 teaspoons nutmeg
  ½ teaspoon salt
1¾ cups molasses
  ½ cup firmly packed dark brown
    sugar
  ¾ cup butter or margarine

1. In large bowl, combine flour, cinnamon, ginger, nutmeg, and salt.
2. In 2-quart saucepan, stir together molasses, brown sugar, and butter. Cook over medium heat, stirring occasionally, until butter is melted and ingredients are well mixed.
3. Pour liquid mixture into flour mixture and stir until well blended.

Note: check specific project directions for special rolling, cutting, and baking instructions before proceeding with this recipe.

4. Form dough into ball and knead until smooth and pliable.
5. Roll out dough on foil-lined cookie sheets to ¼-inch thickness, using lightly floured rolling pin.
6. Cover cookie sheets loosely and refrigerate at least 30 minutes.
7. Cut out cookie pieces, remove and reserve excess dough.
8. Bake in 350°F oven 12 to 15 minutes or until cookies are firm and lightly browned.
9. Cool cookie sheets completely on racks before removing cookie pieces from foil.

BASIC HONEY GINGERBREAD DOUGH

7½ cups unsifted flour
  5 teaspoons ground cinnamon
  1 tablespoon ground ginger
  1 tablespoon baking soda
1½ teaspoons nutmeg
  ½ teaspoon salt
1½ cups butter or margarine
1½ cups firmly packed dark brown
    sugar
  ¾ cup honey
  3 eggs

1. In large bowl, combine flour, cinnamon, ginger, baking soda, nutmeg, and salt.
2. Beat butter in large bowl with electric mixer at medium speed.
3. Add sugar and honey to butter and beat until smooth, then add eggs and beat well.
4. With wooden spoon, beat in flour mixture about a cup at a time until well blended.
5. Cover bowl and refrigerate several hours.

Note: check specific project directions for special rolling, cutting, and baking instructions before proceeding with this recipe.

6. Roll out dough on foil-lined cookie sheets to ¼-inch thickness, using lightly floured rolling pin.
7. Cut out cookie pieces, remove, wrap, and chill excess dough for later use.
8. Bake in 350°F oven 12 to 15 minutes or until cookies are firm and lightly browned.
9. Cool cookie sheets completely on racks before removing cookie pieces from foil.

MIXING THE DOUGH

Gingerbread dough will differ in color depending on the ingredients used. Here is a batch of the darkest dough, using dark brown sugar and dark corn syrup or molasses, and a batch of the lightest, using light brown sugar and light syrup or molasses or honey. Several projects call for two shades of dough, and you can use color differences as a decorative device if you wish.

To make a batch of the Basic Gingerbread Doughs called for in this book (see three recipes later in this chapter), combine flour and other dry ingredients in bowl. Then, if the recipe calls for molasses or corn syrup, heat together remaining ingredients in a saucepan until well mixed. Pour liquid mixture into dry and stir until well blended. The Basic Dough recipe calling for honey is not heated.

3. Cut out cardboard patterns with matte knife or sharp scissors. For most projects, you will need to use tracing paper patterns later to mark design details (see Cutting and Baking, step 6). You can cut out each individual tracing paper pattern or leave the sheet whole.

MAKING THE PATTERNS

1. Tape tracing paper (or any paper you can see through) over pattern printed on page of book, and, using sharp pencil, carefully copy outline and design details inside outline. Here, one pattern has been traced and another is half done. Tape prevents paper from moving as you trace.

2. Transfer pattern outline from tracing paper to lightweight cardboard using dull pencil and carbon paper. Lay cardboard on flat surface, place carbon paper, shiny side down, on top. Position tracing over carbon paper and tape to cardboard before tracing over lines.

Patterns for rectangular construction pieces may be illustrated in reduced size, with the full-sized dimensions given. To rule full-sized patterns, use T-square, triangle, and ruler if you have them, to make exact right angles. Otherwise, use a ruler and graph paper (with a grid printed on it), or a straight-edge ruler and anything with a right angle, like a book cover.

CUTTING AND BAKING

1. Roll out dough on foil-lined cookie sheet with lightly floured rolling pin. Place damp cloth or paper towels on work surface under sheet to prevent sliding.

Individual project instructions may or may not recommend oiling the foil, depending on how much oil the dough contains.

For each project, the instructions specify the thickness to which dough should be rolled out. It's usually ¼ inch, but a few say ¹⁄₁₆ or ½ inch.

2. After dough is rolled to correct thickness, trim with sharp knife to within 1 inch of edge of cookie sheet. For some projects, cookie sheets of specific sizes are recommended. There are no standard sizes, however, and for all but the largest constructions, you can use sheets of any size, although you may not be able to use the layout for cutting out the pieces recommended in the instructions.

3. Dust underside of cardboard patterns very lightly with flour and arrange on dough, leaving about ¼ inch between each. Don't crowd the patterns, but angle them when possible to make the best use of the dough.

Some recipes call for covering rolled-out dough with plastic wrap and refrigerating for 30 minutes or more before cutting out shapes. If you refrigerate overnight, thaw dough before starting to cut it out.

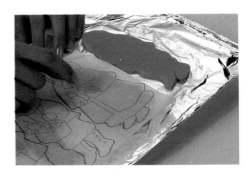

4. Carefully cut around each cardboard pattern with sharp knife. Individual project instructions will tell you how many cookie pieces to cut out of each pattern ("cut 2", for example; no indication means cut just 1).

5. Gently cut away excess dough from around cut-out shapes, using knife to lift edges as you proceed. Knead excess dough together into ball and reserve. Wrap in plastic wrap and refrigerate if you are not going to use it right away.

You may need to reroll excess dough to have enough to cut out all the project pieces.

6. If tracing paper patterns have designs inside outline, position patterns on cut-out cookie pieces. (First cut out pattern around outline if it will be easier to handle that way.) Following the lines of the interior design details, prick holes through patterns into dough with a needle or pin. Then remove the patterns. The pinpricks will show faintly after you bake the pieces and serve as a guide for decorating.

7. All ready to pop in the oven! For the three Basic Gingerbread Dough recipes in this chapter, the cookie pieces are baked in a 350°F oven for 12 to 15 minutes, or until firm and lightly browned. But read the baking instructions specific to each project before proceeding.

To check pieces for size, you can lay the cardboard patterns on them while pieces are still warm (5 minutes out of oven). Trim away parts that have expanded, or gently mold pieces into shape with your fingers.

8. After removing cookie sheets from oven, place on wire rack and cool cookie pieces completely before removing them from sheets. If they need to be cut, shaped, or have holes put through them, do that while they are still warm. They will be cool enough to handle in less than 5 minutes.

9. Remove cookie pieces from foil, lifting them firmly but with care should they stick a bit. Be sure to peel off any remaining foil.

Put the cookie pieces in an airtight, protected container until you are ready to decorate and assemble them. (Pieces can soften and sag if they absorb moisture from air.) Low-sided, medium-sized cardboard boxes with lids work well for storage. Separate the layers of pieces with waxed paper or paper towels.

ROYAL ICING

1. To make Royal Icing, combine 1 pound confectioners sugar, 3 egg whites, and ½ teaspoon cream of tartar in bowl and beat with electric mixer at low speed until blended. Then beat at high speed 7 to 10 minutes. Icing is ready to use when knife drawn through it leaves a clear path which holds its shape.

These quantities make 1 batch, about 2 cups. Do not double recipe. If you need additional icing, make 2 or more separate batches.

2. To tint Royal Icing, divide batch and put into small bowls (disposable plastic bowls are good for this because you need a separate dish for each color icing). Dip tip of toothpick in food coloring and dot on icing.

Icing dries out very quickly, so keep bowls covered with damp cloths, damp paper towels, or plastic wrap even while you are working with them. Do not refrigerate.

3. Use rubber spatula to mix food coloring into Royal Icing, stirring to blend thoroughly. Add more food coloring a bit at a time with a toothpick until you get desired intensity.

It's a good idea to mix all the colors you will need before you start decorating the cookie pieces.

TIPS SHEET

The point of this picture is to show full-size what different metal decorator's tips look like, and what each of them can do. There are more here than most people need. Manufacturers in the U.S. give each one a number. Lower numbers have smaller holes. Starting from upper left, across the top are "writing" tips for piping lines of icing (#1-S, #1 through #9, and #12). The "star" tips with Xs (larger ones are bent inward), starting lower right in yellow, make star-shaped spots or decoratively ridged lines (#13 through #18, and #30). These, and the type with two rows of teeth (#47, lower left), can make many different designs, especially if you turn them as you squeeze. If you stop-and-go as you draw a line of icing, it makes wrinkling folds. Most of the decorative details in this book can be executed with a round writing tip about $1/16$ inch (1.5 mm), a small star tip about $3/16$ inch (5 mm), and the serrated tip shown.

A pastry bag is used for applying decorative icing. These are made of plastic-lined cloth. Disposable bags made of plastic or paper can also be used. A good size is about 10 inches long. A threaded plastic adapter nozzle fits part way through the hole at the tip of the bag. This allows you to change tips without emptying the icing from the bag. The metal tip fits onto the protruding nozzle and is held in place with a plastic coupling ring threaded to match the nozzle.

Icing will stay moist and workable if no air gets to it to dry it out. You can buy a tip cover (yellow, in this photo) with no hole in it to seal off the small end of a bag full of icing. Tightly fold the large end of the bag to seal it off, then you can leave that bag for a while, perhaps to work with another bag filled with icing of a different color. For this reason, it is a good idea to have two or three bags, adapter nozzles with coupling rings, and tip covers.

After you buy a pastry bag, the tip must be snipped off with scissors so the hole is just big enough for half of the threaded rings of the coupler to be

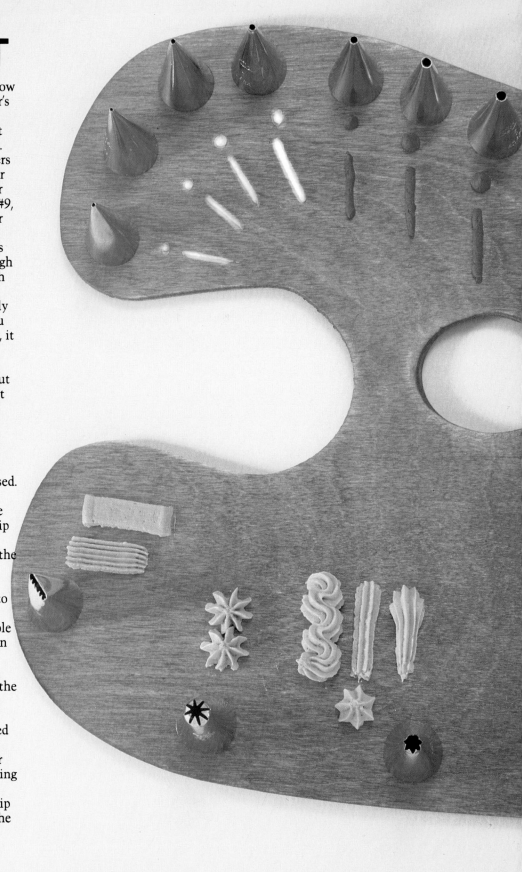

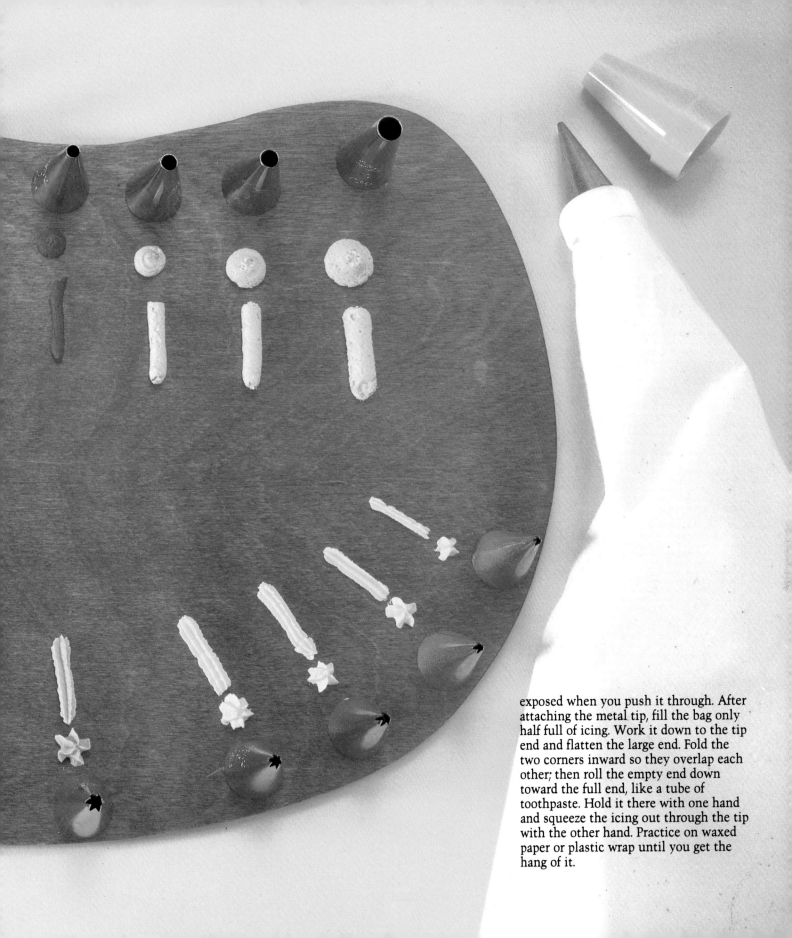

exposed when you push it through. After
attaching the metal tip, fill the bag only
half full of icing. Work it down to the tip
end and flatten the large end. Fold the
two corners inward so they overlap each
other; then roll the empty end down
toward the full end, like a tube of
toothpaste. Hold it there with one hand
and squeeze the icing out through the tip
with the other hand. Practice on waxed
paper or plastic wrap until you get the
hang of it.

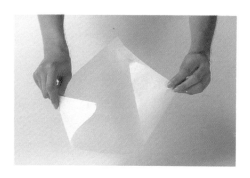

DECORATING

1. Icing is "piped" through metal tips attached to parchment cones or cloth or plastic-lined pastry bags. Disposable parchment paper triangles come in packages of 100 and are inexpensive. They are especially practical if you are using several icing colors, since each color must be applied in a separate container.

To fold a parchment triangle into a cone shape, first hold it in your hands so the point of the triangle is on top.

2. Now bring the other two points together and draw them around to meet the first point. Staple or glue points together. Cut ½ inch off cone tip and fit a metal "writing" tip inside.

If you are using a pastry bag, fit it with an adapter and tip following instructions in Tips Sheet. See Tips Sheet for photographs of different tips and what they do.

3. Using spatula, scoop Royal Icing from bowl into parchment cone. Fill cone about ½ full, working icing towards tip as you proceed.

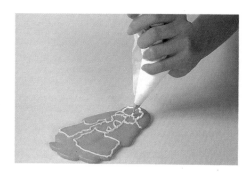

4. Fold three sides of cone down and into cone, leaving a point. Press icing down firmly in tip before you start rolling the top down.

5. Fold point over and over several times (like rolling up a toothpaste tube) to seal icing in cone. Squeeze a little icing through tip to be sure all the air is out before starting to pipe on the design outlines.

6. Outline design details which were marked with pinpricks on cookie pieces before they were baked. The flow of icing from the cone tip is controlled by the pressure of your hand and fingers. You may want to practice on aluminum foil or waxed paper before starting to decorate the cookie pieces.

FLOW FROSTING

1. Use Flow Frosting to cover surfaces within Royal Icing outlines. Stir small amounts of water into bowl of tinted or white Royal Icing until it flows slowly in an even stream, like heavy cream.

2. Roll a parchment cone and cut ¼ inch off the tip. Fill with frosting and gently squeeze a puddle into center of design outlined in icing. Keep bowl of frosting covered with damp cloth or paper towels.

3. The icing acts like a dike around the frosting. Be sure the piped outline of icing has dried hard before filling in with frosting.

Poke frosting into corners with toothpick so area inside icing is completely and evenly filled.

Another technique is simply to dip a knife into the bowl of frosting and let it run down blade into area to be frosted, then work it into corners with point of blade.

Some people like to use an artist's brush to paint frosting directly from bowl onto cookie or to coax it into corners from a puddle in center of design area. Decorate cookie pieces completely and allow them to dry thoroughly before starting to assemble them.

Hint: If you are using two frosting colors in one area, work with only one color at a time, and allow it to dry at least an hour before applying another, so the two will not bleed into each other.

Hint: A super fast-drying alternative to icing is to melt sugar into a hot syrup (until carmelized). Then quickly dip edges of both pieces to be joined in syrup and immediately stick them together. Don't leave pieces in syrup very long, though, or they will soften.

COLOR BLENDING CHART				To produce these additional colors, mix the pro— portions shown.
Green	Yellow	Red	Blue	
—	2	1	—	Orange
—	—	3	1	Purple
1	—	—	3	Turquoise
1	12	—	—	Chartreuse
1	4	3	—	Toast
—	—	1	2	Violet

CONSTRUCTION

Use Royal Icing and a #2 or #3 writing tip to pipe icing onto areas to be "cemented" together. To make a support-stand to attach to the back of a standing figure, cut an appropriate-sized right-angled triangle out of dough, bake, and after figure is decorated, pipe icing on one long edge and attach to back of figure.

1. First join one side wall to one end piece by piping icing along one edge and pressing end of other piece into it. Some instructions suggest you pipe icing onto both surfaces to be joined and pipe a reinforcing strip along inside of corner.

2. The icing must dry hard before joined pieces can be handled. Since this takes 30 minutes to 4 hours, depending on thickness, humidity, stress, etc., prop pieces so they stay together and dry at right angles to each other.

3. When first two pieces have hardened together, attach other end piece or wall. Another technique is to keep setting each new piece inside the next rather than sandwiching the two walls between the two end pieces as shown.

In the instruction text, the words "right" and "left" assume that you are facing the project.

4. When all 4 sides have hardened, pipe icing along one roof-angle of each end piece. You can also pipe icing on underside of roof piece as well. If too much icing squeezes out, scrape off with blade and wipe with moist towel before dry. To chip it off later is more risky, but less likely to leave a smudge.

5. Press roof piece into position and hold by hand briefly so icing begins to set. Prop in position with full food cans and paper towels. Apply frosting, press other roof piece into place, and prop it until dry. Use little dabs of icing to attach doors, shutters, any other cookie trim, and confections.

Old medieval molds were carved into hardwood. The craftsman's chisels dug into the smoothed surface so that soft dough could be rolled into the depression he carved and, when peeled away, reveal something magical—a crusading knight, a mermaid, a unicorn, a rare fruit from a distant land.

The 23 metal cookie cutters on these two pages and the 12 animals on the next page may be traced to make ornaments or scenes for many projects in this book such as "Country Farm," "Noah's Ark," "Haunted House" for Halloween, etc.

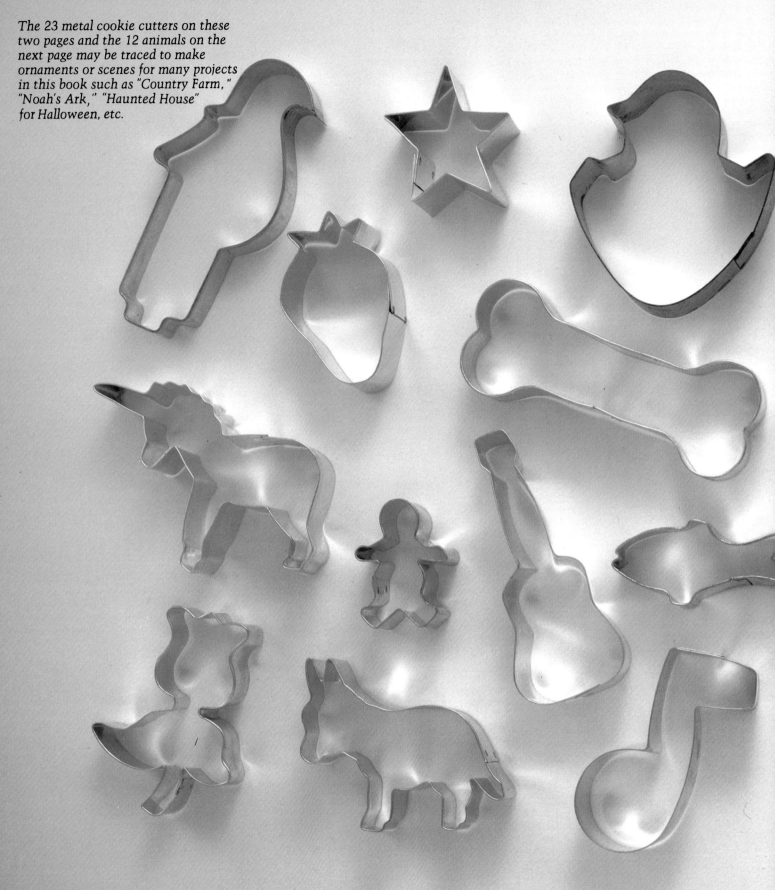

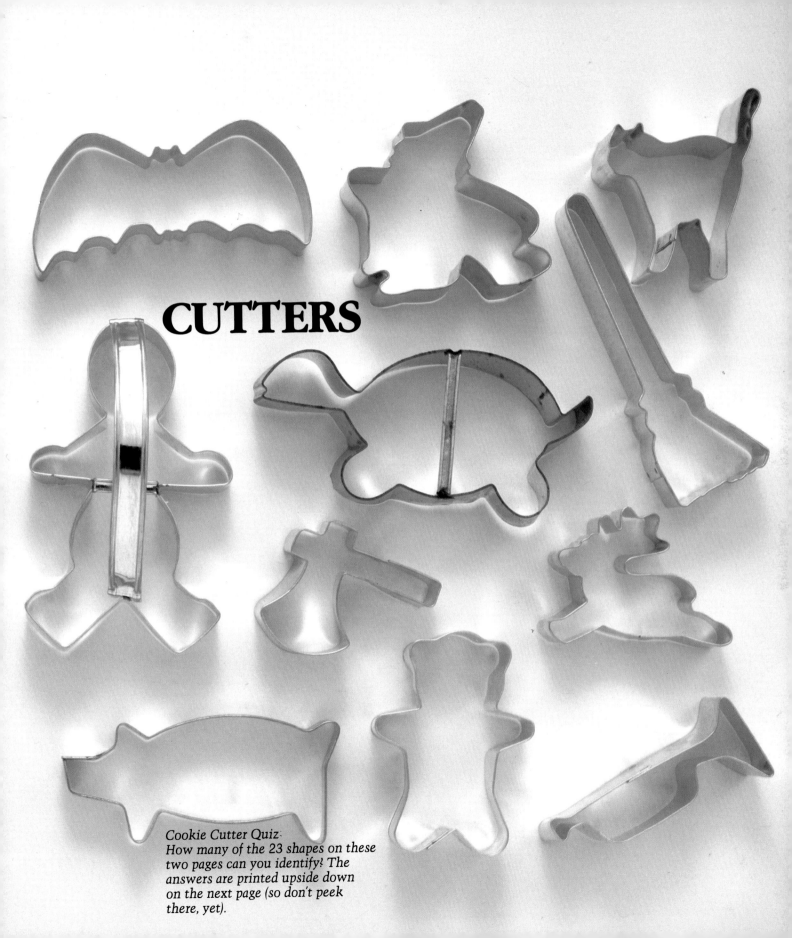

CUTTERS

Cookie Cutter Quiz:
How many of the 23 shapes on these
two pages can you identify! The
answers are printed upside down
on the next page (so don't peek
there, yet).

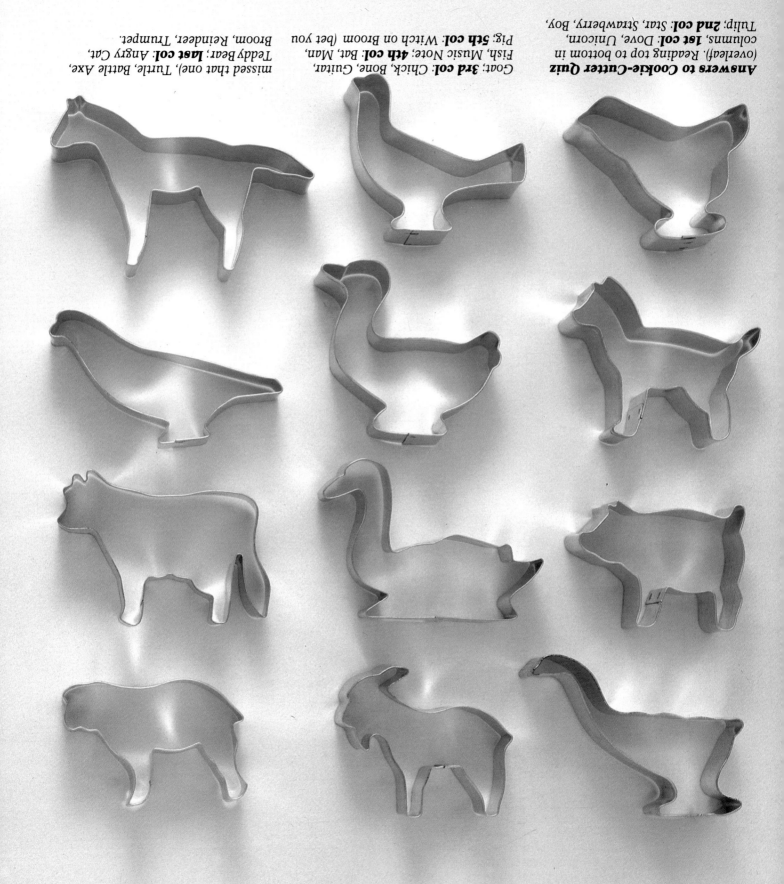

Chopped Candied Fruit

Chocolate-covered Cherries

Jordan Almonds

the candy store

It's not so much the house; it's the goodies on it that make a gingerbread structure memorable. These color pages give names to many candies that you might want to use but haven't a name for.

Small Pectin Drops

Don't be surprised, though, if your candyman calls them by a different name. The same confections are called by different names in different parts of the world, and many of them are imported. Soft, colored-pectin candies, for example, are made in a wide variety of shapes and hues the world over. (The best quality pectin drops are made from apples, incidentally.)

Chocolate Marshmallow Wreath

Nonpareils: with colored seeds

Gum Balls

Chocolate Kisses

Fig Bars

It's usually best to find a good candy store and point to what you want, or even bring this book with you and ask the clerk if he or she has something similar to the confections shown.

Spearmint Leaves

Peppermints

Dutch Mint-Coated
Chocolate Lentils

Swiss Bittersweet
Chocolate
(broken chunks)

Gelatin Sheets

Candy Corn

Chicory Coffee

Swiss Raspberries
and Blueberries

Danish
Chocolate Mint
Lentils

Candy Shot
("Dots")

Cherries

Pectin Fruit Drops
(made from pure
apple jelly)

Chocolate Sprinkles

Honey Horehound
("Pebbles")

French Peppermints

Small Pectin
Buttons

Licorice and
Strawberry Laces (thin)
and Whips (thick)

Edible Glitter

Cinnamon
Hots

Shredded Coconut
(unsweetened)

Chocolate
Filled
Straws

Peppercorns

Gum Drops

Turkish Delight
("Lakoum")

Flaked Coconut
(sweetened)

Belgian
Rock-Crystal
Candy

Fruit Flavored
Hard Candies

Chinese
Crystalized Ginger

Licorice
Diamonds
("Easy Aces")

Chopped Walnuts

Candy Sticks

Wild Rice

Silver Dragees

Fruit Slices

Left to right, first row: Front and side views of "The Candy Cathedral," covered with fruit-centered cookies, studded with red-hots, and decorated with candy canes and fruit slices. *Below:* "Cookie Hall," a European town building. *Below, right:* "Candy Cottage." *Bottom left:* "The Washington House," a replica of an 18th century hostelry. *Bottom right:* An authentic "Bavarian Chalet." The thick walls and chunky, romanticized style are typical of the Austrian Tyrol.

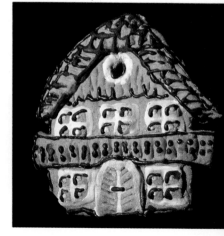

Real Estate

These two pages are a place to shop for ideas to incorporate into your own gingerbread houses. These represent some traditional and some unusually ambitious state-of-the-art structures.

Above: *"Victorian Brick" is a prize-winning copy of the mansion occupied by the governor of the state of Indiana, U.S.A. The detailed piping of the bricks, decorative swags, windows above and around the door, and the front walk make this an outstanding example of the American style of replica structures.* ***Left:*** *Pretzel-stick logs and nonpareil "slate" roof tiles cover the gingerbread structure of a chalet. Without the peppermint trim and front entrance columns, it might be a log cabin or rustic barn.*

161

RECIPES

**from the Past and Present
the World Over**

Recipes From the Past

The following recipes are selected from various times and places in gingerbread's rich history. For that reason, some may no longer work because the chemical and other properties of the ingredients may have changed since the recipe was first recorded. And remember, written instructions for recipes were much less complete in the old days.

NOTTINGHAM FAIR BRANDY SNAPS

On the first Thursday in October, in ancient times, thousands of geese were driven into Nottingham for the fair, each flock under the guidance of a gooseherd, armed with a crook. People attended the fair from all parts of the English Midlands, since this was the proper occasion for selecting the Christmas geese.

Brandy snaps, although sold at other fairs throughout England, are so characteristic of this particular fair that people seldom refer to it without remarking nostalgically, "Brandy snaps, curled like cones! We always ate them at Nottingham Goose Fair!"

1½ cups butter
1½ cups sugar
1 cup molasses
3 cups sifted flour
4 teaspoons ground ginger

Heat butter, sugar, and molasses until well blended. Add ginger. Remove mixture from stove and add flour, a little at a time, beating after each addition. Roll out, cut into 3-inch round wafers, and bake at 350°F for 12 to 15 minutes. When done and cooled on a rack just enough to handle, you can quickly curl them into cones and let them cool thoroughly.

PAIN D'EPICE
A spiced bread from France

1¼ cups boiling water
1 teaspoon anise seed
1 cup honey
1¼ cups sugar
½ teaspoon baking soda
¼ cup rum (optional) (use 1½ cups of water if rum is omitted)
4 cups sifted flour
2½ teaspoons baking powder
1 teaspoon ground cinnamon
½ teaspoon ground ginger
¼ teaspoon salt
3 tablespoons chopped candied citron
3 tablespoons chopped candied orange peel
½ teaspoon grated orange rind
¼ cup chopped almonds (optional)

Bring water to boil with anise seed. Add honey and sugar and stir until dissolved. Remove from heat and stir in soda and rum or water. Set aside. Preheat oven to 350°F. Sift together flour, baking powder, cinnamon, ginger, and salt. Add honey mixture to dry ingredients and beat until smooth. Add fruit (and nuts) and mix well. Turn mixture into two 9 x 5 x 3-inch greased (or buttered) loaf pans and bake about 1 hour, or until done.

NUREMBERG GINGERBREAD
The bakers of Nuremberg, Germany, have been famous for their spiced cookies and gingerbread since the 16th century.

4 eggs
9 ounces sugar
2½ ounces candied orange peels
2½ ounces candied lemon peels, cut finely
2½ ounces shelled almonds, cut finely
9 ounces flour
1 teaspoon cinnamon
1 teaspoon ground ginger
1 generous pinch clove powder
1 pinch mace
1 pinch cardamom
1 teaspoon salt
1 teaspoon baking powder
Big baking wafers

Beat together eggs and sugar until foamy. Add orange and lemon peels and almonds. Then add rest of ingredients. Lay wafers on top of baking pan and spread dough on top of them. Cut out cookies and let them dry off overnight. Next day, put in preheated oven with the door ajar. Bake until light brown, in electric oven at 300 to 375°F, in gas oven at 300 to 325°F. Frost when still warm, if desired, with Rum or Chocolate Frosting.
Yield: 30 to 40 cookies

Rum Frosting
  7 ounces confectioners sugar
  2 to 3 tablespoons rum or lemon juice

Sift sugar and mix in smoothly with liquid.

Chocolate Frosting
  7 ounces confectioners sugar
  3 tablespoons powdered cocoa
  3 tablespoons water
  1 tablespoon coconut butter

Mix sugar and cocoa first, then add water and coconut butter.

DOUGH FOR GINGERBREAD MOLDS
  1 cup soft butter
  1 cup sugar
  ¼ cup ginger
  1 teaspoon cinnamon
  1 teaspoon baker's cocoa
  ⅛ teaspoon salt
  ¾ cup dark molasses
  1 cup evaporated milk
  1 teaspoon vanilla
  ½ teaspoon lemon extract
  5½ cups sifted flour

Cream butter. Sift together, then add sugar, spices, cocoa, and salt; cream until mixture is fluffy. Add molasses, milk, vanilla and lemon extracts; beat to blend until mixture looks curdled. Blend in flour, a little at a time, beating to keep mixture smooth. Cover dough lightly and refrigerate 2 hours or freeze ¼ hour. Butter the wooden mold, then sprinkle flour onto it and tap mold so it is dusted evenly. Preheat oven to 325°F. Roll small amount of chilled dough into mold and trim to form. If dough becomes sticky, chill again before rolling. Rest mold at an angle on ungreased cookie sheet, loosen cookie at base and guide to sheet. Bake 15 minutes. Slide cookies onto rack to cool.

ELIZABETHAN GINGERBREAD
Here's an authentic 17th-century recipe for molded gingerbread:

  3 grated stale manchets (a manchet is fine white bread)
  Ginger
  Cinnamon
  Liquorice
  Aniseed
  Sugar

Boil all these ingredients together in a quart of claret until they form a stiff paste. Work the paste, then roll it out thinly. After dusting the molds with rice flour, press the paste into them, and cut it level across the top of the mold. Finally turn it out and dry it in the oven.

HOT SPICE-GINGERBREAD.

Hot Spice-Gingerbread, hot ! hot ! all hot !

This noisy fellow loudly bawls,

Hot ! hot ! hot ! smoking hot ! red hot !

In every street or public place he calls.

GINGERBREAD ROYAL

From the cookbook used at Mount Vernon comes a recipe for fancy-cut gingerbread belonging to Frances Parke Custis, Martha Washington's mother-in-law.

    2 cups blanched almonds
      Rose water (see Colonial Soft
      Gingerbread with Rose Water
      recipe in this chapter).
    2 cups sifted confectioners sugar
    ½ teaspoon ground cinnamon
    1 tablespoon candied ginger
    ½ cup chopped dates
    ½ cup raisins

Beat almonds in a mortar and mix with two tablespoons rose water as they are prepared. Stir in sugar, spices, and fruit, using enough additional rose water to form a very stiff paste. Roll out on board dusted with confectioners sugar and cut into fancy shapes. Set in a cool oven to dry out.

LAFAYETTE GINGERBREAD

Another fancy gingerbread recipe came from Elizabeth Raffold in 1795. This was named for the Marquis de Lafayette.

"Five eggs.
Half a pound of brown sugar.
Half a pound of fresh butter.
A pint of sugar-house molasses.
A pound and a half of flour.
Four table-spoonfuls of ginger.
Two large sticks of cinnamon.
Three dozen grains of allspice.
Three dozen of cloves, powdered and
  sifted
The juice and grated peel of two large
  lemons.

Stir the butter and sugar to a cream. Beat the eggs very well. Pour the molasses, at once, into the butter and sugar. Add the ginger and other spice, and stir all well together. Put in the egg and flour alternately, stirring all the time. Stir the whole very hard, and put in the lemon at the last. When the whole is mixed, stir it till very light. Butter an earthen pan, or a thick tin or iron one, and put the gingerbread in it. Bake it in a moderate oven, an hour or more, according to its thickness. Take care that it does not burn."

MUSTER DAY GINGERBREAD

Muster Day, the first Tuesday in June, was a day of compulsory militia training for the men of New England— and a day of revelry for the entire family when the training was done. Gingerbread was an essential part of the menu.

    ⅔ cup molasses
    ⅔ cup brown sugar
    2 teaspoons ground ginger
    ½ teaspoon ground cinnamon
    ¼ teaspoon ground cloves
    2 teaspoons baking soda
    ⅔ cup butter
    1 egg
    5 cups flour

Heat molasses, brown sugar, ginger, cinnamon, and cloves to boiling point. Remove from heat and add baking soda, then pour over butter in a mixing bowl. Stir until butter has melted, then add egg and flour and mix thoroughly. Knead for a few minutes, then gather dough into ball. Refrigerate dough until firm enough to roll easily, then roll on lightly floured board and cut with cookie cutters. Place on greased sheet and bake at 325°F for 10 minutes. Remove small cookies from sheet as they brown.

SAILOR'S GINGERBREAD

Sailors loved gingerbread as much as landlubbers did. This recipe was published in the New England *Vineyard Gazette* in August, 1857.

Sift two pounds of flour (8 cups) into a bowl, and cut into it 1¼ pounds fresh butter; rub the butter well into the flour and then mix in a pint of West Indian molasses and a pound of the best brown sugar. Beat eight eggs until very light. Stir into the eggs a gill, or ½ cup, of brandy. Add also to the egg ½ cup of ground ginger and a tablespoonful of powdered cinnamon, with 1 teaspoon of baking soda melted in a little warm water. Moisten the flour with this mixture until it becomes a soft dough. Sprinkle a little flour on your pastry board, and with a broad knife spread portions of the mixture thickly and smoothly upon it. The thickness must be equal all

through; therefore spread it carefully and evenly, as the dough will be too soft to roll out. Then with the edge of a tumbler dipped in flour, cut it out into round cakes. Have ready square pans, lightly buttered; lay the cakes in them sufficiently apart to prevent their ruining each other when baked. Set the pans into a brisk oven and bake the cakes well, seeing that they do not burn.

COLONIAL SOFT GINGERBREAD WITH ROSE WATER

by Amelia Simmons, 1796
"Rub two pounds of sugar, one pound of butter, into four pounds of flour, add eight eggs, one ounce ginger, one pint milk, four spoons rose water, knead dough until stiff, shape to one's fancy, bake in a pan 15 minutes." (Bake in moderate oven, 350°F.)

Rose Water
If the druggist doesn't have it, this is how it was made. Place a peck of freshly picked, red or crimson rose petals into a quart of spring water. Distill it twice over a low fire before corking it loosely and letting it stand 3 days. On the fourth day, fasten down the cork and let it age.

SOUTHERN SORGHUM GINGERBREAD

If the New Englanders used West Indies molasses and rum and maple syrup for their gingerbread, Southerners substituted something of their own: sorghum, the sugary residue left when cane is cut down, milled, pressed, and cooked each fall. More than one southerner remembers a mother dipping a teacup into the stone crock of sorghum molasses in preparation for a batch of hot, fresh gingerbread on a cool autumn evening.

    2 cups flour
    1 teaspoon baking soda
    1¼ teaspoon cream of tartar
    ½ teaspoon cloves
    1 tablespoon ground ginger
    1 teaspoon cinnamon
    ½ teaspoon salt
    ½ cup butter
    ½ cup lard
    1 cup hot water

2 eggs, beaten
1½ cups sorghum molasses

In a large mixing bowl sift flour, soda, cream of tartar, cloves, ginger, cinnamon, and salt. Mix the lard and butter in the hot water and when melted, pour into the flour mixture. Stir well, then add beaten eggs. Continue stirring, add molasses, and stir well again. Spoon the batter into the buttered and floured baking pan. Set to bake in a preheated 350°F oven for 35 to 40 minutes.

NEW ENGLAND MAPLE SYRUP GINGERBREAD

    1 cup maple syrup
    1 cup sour cream
    1 egg, well beaten
 2½ cups flour
 1½ teaspoons soda
    2 teaspoons ground ginger
    ½ teaspoon salt
    ½ cup melted butter

Combine the maple syrup, cream, and egg, and mix well. Sift the dry ingredients and stir into the liquid mixture, beating well. Add butter and beat thoroughly. Pour into buttered 9-inch square baking pan and bake in a 350°F oven for 30 minutes. Serve with whipped cream sprinkled with shaved maple sugar.

RUM GINGERBREAD

    ½ cup sugar
    ½ cup butter
    1 egg
 2½ cups flour
 1¾ teaspoons baking soda
    1 cup molasses
    ¾ cup hot water
    ¼ cup rum
    1 teaspoon ground ginger
    ½ teaspoon cinnamon
    ¼ teaspoon cloves

Combine butter and sugar with egg and beat well. Sift flour and soda and add to first mixture alternately with the molasses, water, and rum. Add spices. Pour batter into a buttered 9 x 12-inch pan and bake at 350°F for 45 minutes. Serve with whipped cream. Buttermilk may be substituted for the water and rum.

Just Plain Good Recipes From All Over

"I don't s'pose anybody on earth likes gingerbread better'n I do and gets less'n I do."

A. Lincoln

BUTTERMILK GINGERBREAD

    ¼ cup softened butter
    ½ cup firmly packed brown sugar
    1 egg
    ½ cup molasses
 1½ cups unbleached all purpose flour
    1 teaspoon baking soda
    1 teaspoon ground ginger
    1 teaspoon ground cinnamon
    ½ cup buttermilk
       Lace paper doily
       Confectioners sugar

Combine butter, sugar, egg, and molasses and beat with an electric mixer until light and fluffy. Mix flour well with soda and spices. Add alternately with buttermilk to molasses mixture, beginning and ending with dry ingredients. Pour into greased 8-inch square pan. Bake at 350°F for 30 minutes. Cool on rack in pan. When cooled, lay a lace paper doily on top of gingerbread and, using a fine strainer, sprinkle top with sifted confectioners sugar. To remove doily, lift it straight up so you don't disturb the pattern you have made with sugar. To serve, cut into pieces.
Yield: 6 to 8 servings

GINGERBREAD CAKE

Many people consider it to be a cake, but in the old days it was meant to be a bread served at lunch or dinner with sweet butter. It is best served slightly warm with plenty of butter. If cold, cut it, then spread with softened butter.

    ¾ cup shortening
    ¾ cup brown sugar
    2 eggs
    ⅔ cup molasses
 2½ cups flour
    2 teaspoons baking soda
    2 teaspoons ground ginger
 1½ teaspoons ground cinnamon
    ½ teaspoon ground cloves
    ½ teaspoon ground nutmeg
    ½ teaspoon baking powder
    ¾ teaspoon salt
    1 cup boiling water

Cream shortening, add brown sugar, then eggs and molasses. Sift dry ingredients together and add slowly. Mix well and, lastly, add boiling water. Bake at 375°F in a greased and floured 9 x 13-inch pan for 30 to 35 minutes.

MOIST OLD-FASHIONED GINGERBREAD

It's the extra molasses and the boiling water that make this recipe so moist and so memorable.

    1 cup light or dark molasses
    ½ cup boiling water
    5 tablespoons butter
    ½ teaspoon salt
 1½ to 2 teaspoons ground ginger
    1 teaspoon baking soda
    2 cups all purpose flour

Put molasses in a mixing bowl, add boiling water and butter and stir until well mixed. Add salt, ginger, and soda and stir lightly. Then stir in just enough flour to moisten and mix ingredients. Turn into a 9 x 9 x 2-inch baking pan. Bake at 375°F for 25 to 35 minutes, or until top springs back when pressed lightly and bread pulls away from sides of pan. Serve as is, with butter, or with a sauce.
Yield: 6 servings

CLASSIC GINGERBREAD CAKE

2½ cups flour
1½ teaspoons baking soda
1 teaspoon cinnamon
1 teaspoon ground ginger
½ teaspoon salt
½ teaspoon ground cloves
1 cup molasses
½ cup sugar
½ cup butter
1 egg, well beaten
1 cup boiling water

In large mixing bowl, combine flour, soda, cinnamon, ginger, salt, and cloves. In medium-sized bowl, combine molasses, sugar, butter, and egg, and mix until well blended. With electric mixer set at medium speed, gradually add molasses mixture to flour mixture and beat until smooth. Then add boiling water and mix until well blended. Pour batter into greased and floured 9 x 9 x 2-inch square baking pan. Bake 55 to 60 minutes or until cake tester or toothpick inserted into center comes out clean. Cool cake in pan on wire rack, then cut into nine 3 x 3 x 3-inch squares. Top cake with sauce. Can be served warm or at room temperature.

HARD SAUCE

4 tablespoons butter, softened
1 cup confectioners sugar
½ teaspoon vanilla or lemon extract
1 egg white

Cream butter, gradually add sugar and extract. Beat egg white until stiff and add to sugar mixture, beating until fluffy. Pile lightly in serving dish and chill.
Yield: 6 servings

BLUEBERRY HARD SAUCE

¼ cup butter
1 cup confectioners sugar
½ cup crushed blueberries
1 egg white

Cream butter until soft. Gradually beat in sugar, then blueberries. Add egg white and beat until light. Pile lightly in serving dish and chill until cold, but not hard.
Yield: 1 cup or 4 to 6 servings.

CUSTARD SAUCE

3 cups milk
2 egg yolks, slightly beaten
¾ cup sugar
1½ tablespoons cornstarch
¼ teaspoon salt
1 teaspoon vanilla

Bring 2½ cups of the milk to boil over medium heat in heavy 2-quart saucepan. In medium-sized bowl, add egg yolks to remaining ½ cup milk and stir until well blended. Stir sugar, cornstarch, and salt into egg mixture until smooth. Stir about 1 cup boiling milk into cornstarch and egg mixture, then stir all into remaining hot milk in saucepan. Without letting mixture boil, continue cooking, stirring constantly, about 2 minutes or until thickened. Remove from heat and stir in vanilla.
Yield: about 3 cups

LEMON SAUCE

¾ cup sugar
3 tablespoons flour
1¼ cups boiling water
1 egg yolk
2 tablespoons butter
1 teaspoon grated lemon rind
3 tablespoons lemon juice
⅛ teaspoon salt

Combine sugar and flour in top of double boiler. Add boiling water gradually, stirring constantly. Cook over hot water until thick and smooth. Add egg yolk, lemon juice, grated rind, and butter. Mix well and remove from fire. Serve hot or cold.
Yield: about 1½ cups of sauce

QUICK LEMON SAUCE

½ cup sugar
2 tablespoons cornstarch
Dash of salt
1 cup water
2 tablespoons margarine
1 teaspoon grated lemon rind
Juice of 1 lemon

In medium-sized saucepan, combine sugar, cornstarch, and salt. Gradually stir in water. Stirring constantly, bring to boil over medium heat and boil 1

minute. Remove from heat and stir in margarine, lemon rind, and lemon juice.
Yield: about 1½ cups

INDIAN GINGER PUDDING

Indian pudding is a traditional New England and New York state dessert. The dominant ingredients are corn meal—originally ground from maize cultivated by native Americans and grown by the early settlers of the United States—and molasses. Then, whatever spices could be had were added to excite the palate.

1 cup self-rising flour
1½ cups corn meal
½ teaspoon salt
1 teaspoon baking soda
1 teaspoon ground cinnamon
½ teaspoon ground nutmeg
2 teaspoons ground ginger
1 cup seeded raisins, cut in pieces
½ cup sour milk
¾ cup molasses
4 tablespoons melted butter or shortening
Boiling water

Sift flour, corn·meal, salt, soda, and spices together. Add raisins. Combine milk, molasses, and butter and add to dry ingredients. Mix thoroughly. Turn into well greased tube pan or mold. Fill mold not more than ⅔ full. Cover with waxed paper and tie securely. Set mold on rack in large kettle. Pour in boiling water to half the depth of mold. Steam 2 to 2½ hours, depending on depth of mold. Serve with Hard Sauce.
Yield: 6 to 8 servings

GINGER-MOLASSES COOKIES

These soft cookies taste more of molasses than of ginger. The recipe calls for 2 to 6 cups of flour, depending on how flat or how puffy you like the cookies. Experiment with a few mini-batches by pouring some batter into 2 or 3 small bowls and mixing a little more flour into each. Then bake a couple of cookies from each bowl of batter, and from the main bowl, to see how you like them best.

2 to 6 cups of flour
1 teaspoon salt

2 teaspoons ground ginger
2 teaspoons ground cinnamon
½ teaspoon ground cloves
¼ teaspoon ground nutmeg
1 cup sugar
1 cup butter or margarine, softened
1 teaspoon baking soda
1 cup molasses
1 cup sour milk

Mix flour, salt, and spices. Blend in sugar and butter. Mix baking soda into molasses and blend. Stir both mixtures together. Heat sour milk in a pan until hot, but don't let it simmer. Combine with flour-molasses mixture and stir to combine thoroughly. Cool. Roll out, if you used enough flour, or simply drop batter a teaspoon at a time onto greased cookie sheet. Bake at 400°F for 10 to 12 minutes.
Yield: about 4 dozen

GINGERSNAPS
¾ cup shortening
1 cup sugar
¼ cup molasses
1 beaten egg
2 cups flour
2 teaspoons baking soda
½ teaspoon salt
1 teaspoon ground cinnamon
½ teaspoon ground cloves
1 teaspoon ground ginger

Cream shortening and sugar. Add molasses and egg. Beat well. Sift dry ingredients, then add to creamed mixture. Mix well. Roll in small balls. Place 2 inches apart on greased cookie sheet. Bake at 375°F for 10 minutes.
Yield: 4 dozen

GINGERBREAD WAFFLES
If you haven't time to make the waffles from scratch like this, add molasses, baking soda, and ground ginger to your favorite mix and reduce the liquid to ½ cup.

2 cups self-rising flour
2 teaspoons ground ginger
½ teaspoon salt
2 eggs, separated
1 teaspoon baking soda
1 cup molasses
½ cup milk
⅓ cup butter, melted

Sift flour, ginger, and salt together. Combine well beaten egg yolks, soda, and molasses. Add to flour mixture alternately with milk, beating until smooth. Add melted butter and beat well. Fold in stiffly beaten egg whites. Pour ½ cup of batter into hot waffle iron and bake until steam stops. This is a tender, delicate waffle and should be removed from iron in sections. Serve hot with bacon and baked apple, or as a dessert with orange marmalade.
Yield: about 8 waffles

CONSTRUCTION GINGERBREAD
There are 3 recipes for construction dough in the Basic Skills chapter. They call for butter or margarine. This is another reliable construction dough recipe made with solid shortening instead of butter or margarine, and it is recommended, with minor variations, by many experienced gingerbread house-builders.

1 cup solid white shortening
2 cups old-fashioned molasses
½ cup warm water
7 cups all purpose flour
¼ cup sugar
1 teaspoon baking soda
3 teaspoons baking powder
3 teaspoons ground ginger
1 teaspoon ground cinnamon
1 teaspoon salt

Melt shortening and add molasses and ½ cup warm water. Mix in dry ingredients until smooth. If necessary, knead last of flour into dough until smooth and flexible. Chill, then roll dough to about ⅛-inch thickness on cookie sheets. Cut out patterns, remove excess dough from cookie sheets, and bake in 350°F oven about 12 minutes. Makes a medium-sized house with 8 x 6-inch sides, 9½ x 8-inch front and back, and two 10 x 7-inch roof pieces.

VERY MULLED WINE
1 cup water
1 cup sugar (less if you use a sweet wine)
2 sticks cinnamon
2 dozen whole cloves (or fewer depending on your taste)
2 tablespoons ground ginger
1 quart orange juice
3½ liters (about 4 quarts) dry red wine
1 lemon
1 orange

Bring water, sugar, and spices to boil. Remove from heat and let steep for 10 minutes, then strain. Heat orange juice and wine and pour into strained mixture. Cut lemon and orange into thin slices and float one of each in each serving.

CHILDREN'S PUNCH AND JUDY
Fresh strawberries
Holly leaves (optional)
¼ cup minced candied ginger
4 cups cranberry juice, very cold
1 pint lemon or lime sherbet

Freeze whole strawberries, with their tops on, into ice cubes. Holly leaves can be added with them. Mix minced ginger into sherbet. Scrape out balls of sherbet with ice cream scoop and drop them into cold cranberry juice. Pour over strawberry ice cubes.

EGGNOG
12 eggs, separated
1 cup sugar
1½ cups bourbon, rum, or whiskey
6 cups milk
1¼ teaspoons ground nutmeg
1 teaspoon ginger
1 cup heavy or whipping cream

Beat together egg yolks and sugar using electric mixer at low speed. Then, at high speed, beat for 15 minutes until thick and lemon-colored. Scrape bowl frequently. Add whiskey slowly, stirring continuously.

Cover bowl and chill until approximately 20 minutes before serving. Place a 5- or 6-quart punch bowl in refrigerator to chill.

Stir mixture, then pour into chilled punch bowl, adding milk and spices.

Beat egg whites in small bowl with mixer until they form stiff peaks.

In a separate small bowl, beat cream with mixer until it forms stiff peaks.

Gently fold egg whites and cream into mixture using wire whisk.

Sprinkle additional nutmeg on top.

MAIL-ORDER RESOURCES

The following categories of materials and utensils referred to in this book may be ordered from the sources listed on this page.

Baking sheets: cookie and strudel
Cake molds and pans
Candies
Carved wooden boards, molds and
    rollers: springerle and speculatius
Cookie cutters and rollers
Imported confections
Metal tips for decorative icing
Pastry bags: parchment, cloth,
    plastic-lined
Plastic couplings for decorator's tips
Preserved fruits
Spices and herbs

MID-WEST
Buchholtz Import/Export, Inc.
Bavarian Village
8397 East 13-Mile Road
Warren, Michigan 48093
(313) 268-0410

WEST
Ernie's Deli
8400 8th Avenue
Inglewood, California 90305
Telephone orders: (213) 752-8194
Free catalog